Sabine Baring-Gould, R. R Chope, Herbert Stephen Irons

**Carols**

for use in church during Christmas and Epiphany

Sabine Baring-Gould, R. R Chope, Herbert Stephen Irons

**Carols**
*for use in church during Christmas and Epiphany*

ISBN/EAN: 9783337383312

Printed in Europe, USA, Canada, Australia, Japan

Cover: Foto ©Lupo / pixelio.de

More available books at **www.hansebooks.com**

# CAROLS FOR USE IN CHURCH

### During Christmas and Epiphany.

BY

R. R. CHOPE, M.A.,
VICAR OF S. AUGUSTINE'S SOUTH KENSINGTON, ETC.

THE MUSIC EDITED BY
HERBERT STEPHEN IRONS,
*Late Organist of Southwell Minster, &c.*

WITH AN INTRODUCTION BY
S. BARING-GOULD, M.A.,
*Rector of Lew-Trenchard, Author of "The Lives of the Saints," &c.*

---

LONDON:
METZLER & CO., GREAT MARLBOROUGH STREET,
NOVELLO, EWER, & CO., 1, BERNERS STREET.

*Entered at Stationers' Hall.*] [*All rights reserved.*

LONDON:
WILLIAM CLOWES AND SONS, LIMITED, TYPE-MUSIC AND GENERAL PRINTERS,
STAMFORD STREET AND CHARING CROSS.

# CHRISTMAS CAROLS.

In the 11th and 12th centuries, the South of Europe was deeply infected with Manicheism. The Paul'cians, expelled Asia Minor by the Empress Theodora, in A.D. 842, settled in Bulgaria, among the valleys of the Hæmus. Bulgaria became permeated by them. Bulgarian Christianity disappeared under them, never again to acquire active life. The swarm of heretics increased in the absence of persecution, and, through conversion of the semi-Christianised natives. Bulgaria could not contain them or their doctrine. A stream forced a way round the head of the Adriatic, and spread over Northern Italy and Southern France. In the 11th century scarce a city in Italy was free from a colony of Manicheans; the country-people were deeply infected with their doctrine. At the accession of Innocent III., Manicheism was almost undisputed master of Southern France. In Italy it was called Paterinism; in Provence, Albigensianism. In the meantime another stream had entered Germany, and troubled the empire.* The Beghards (a corruption of Bulgarian), carried their doctrine through Northern Europe, and laid the seeds of the revolt of the Hussites under Zisca with the Flail.

Western Manicheism, whether that of the Patarines, Albigenses, or Beghards,† held that matter was evil; the world, the flesh, were the work of the Demiurge, the maker of this world, and God of the Jews and of the Old Testament, and therefore with no good in them; whereas the Gospel was

---

\* Their Greek origin is distinctly asserted: "Illi vero qui combusti sunt (those at Cologne) dixerunt nobis in defensione suâ, hanc hæresin usque ad hæc tempora occultatam fuisse a temporibus martyrum in Græcia." Muratori Antiq., Ital. v. 83.

† "All these he distinguished by the common name of Bulgares, whether they were Paternians, Jovinians, or Albigenses." Matt., Paris, sub. ann. 1238.

the revelation of the Good God, who was the author of spirit. The fall of man was the entrance of soul into relation with body; the emancipation of the soul from its carnal chain was salvation. In such a religion the Incarnation had no real place; and we find, accordingly, that the Flesh-taking of the Word was formally denied by all the sects of Manicheism throughout Europe. Christianity in Southern France had disappeared before Manicheism. It was professed only by the clergy and a few followers; nobles and common people were united in their profession of the Duality of Matter and Spirit, in the opposition of the God of the Creation to the God of the Gospel. Italy was threatened with the same apostacy. The sword of the Crusaders, under Simon de Montfort, swept it out of Provence. A more peaceful band of Crusaders marched against the heretics in Italy, and overcame them. This band was called forth by the great Francis of Assisi. His great community ramifying through every class, by means of the Third Order, caught all earnest religious souls, and bound them by enthusiasm to his Rule. The tide which had set in this direction of Paterinism turned and flowed into the Franciscan Order, which met the peculiar wants and prejudices of those whom Manicheism had previously enticed, in a very remarkable manner.*

S. Francis could not fail to be struck with the necessity of bringing home to the hearts and imagination of the vulgar the great doctrine of the Incarnation. This was the foundation-stone of Christianity. It was because they stood loosely upon it, that the people had fallen such a ready prey to Manicheism. The Incarnation had been set forth by theologians, for the commonly-taught orthodox, in the sublime song of the "Quicunque vult;" it must be brought down to the level of the lowest, if they were to grasp it with unshaken enthusiasm. He had brooded over this difficulty for some time. At last he saw his way out of it. In the winter of 1223, S. Francis was at Rome, seeking the confirmation of his Rule. On the 29th of November, the Order was santioned in full form, by Honorius III., by

---

* The Franciscan Order suffered in the long run from the influx of half-converted Manichees, who formed in its ranks a great schism, constituting the body of the Fraticelli—heretics who had to be put down by very summary means.

Papal Bull, and letters commendatory to all the bishops of Christendom. Then, when Francis had received the confirmation of his life's work, he fell at the feet of the Pope, and made one more request, and that of a different character. He asked to be allowed to introduce into churches, which he was permitted to use, certain ceremonies at Christmas, which had suggested themselves to him as likely to seize upon the popular imagination, and impress the unlearned folk in a way which sermons and catechisms were unable to effect. This also was granted him.

When he made this petition, he was bound for the village of Grecia, a little place not far from Assisi, where he was to spend Christmas.

What follows shall be told in the words of his latest English biographer: *—

"In this village, when the eve of the Nativity approached, Francis instructed a certain grave and worthy man, called Giovanni, to prepare an ox and an ass, along with a manger and all the common fittings of a stable, for his use, in the church. When the solemn night arrived, Francis and his brethren arranged all these things into a visible representation of the occurrences of the night at Bethlehem. The manger was filled with hay, the animals were led into their places; the scene was prepared as we see it now through the churches of Southern Italy—a reproduction, so far as the people knew how, in startling realistic detail, of the surroundings of the first Christmas. And it may be interesting to the modern traveller to know, when he looks on at the quaint Christmas celebration of the Ara Cœli at Rome, or is led with fond pride by some poor Italian through a succession of narrow lanes to see the Præsepio (or cradle) in the parish church or convent chapel, that the scene on which he looks is an appeal to the popular imagination first originated by Francis in the church of his Umbrian village six hundred years ago.

"The original occurrence is full of that honest and literal simplicity which pervades every scene in which we find the humble apostle. The population of the neighbourhood rose as one man to the characteristic call. They gathered round the village church with tapers and torches, making luminous the December night. The brethren within the church, and the crowds of the faithful who came and went with their lights, in and out of the darkness, poured out their hearts in praises to God; and the friars sang new canticles, which were listened to with all the eagerness of a people accustomed to wandering jougleurs and minstrels, and to whom such songs were all the food to be had for the intellect and imagination. No doubt the mystic songs of Francis were among those sacred ballads; and that in the crowd there were many who could take up the chorus of the glowing hymn, 'In fuoco amor mi mise' ('Love sets my heart on fire'), or could answer in those oft-repeated refrains, 'Amor, amor, Jesu,' in the words which the Brothers Minor were used to sing about the rural ways. In the midst of

---

* Mrs. Oliphant, "S. Francis of Assisi," *Macmillan*, p. 223-4.

this glowing and agitated scene, Francis himself stood rapt by the side of the manger, in which his faith could picture to itself the first cradle of his Lord. . . . We are told that Francis stood by this, his simple theatrical (for such, indeed, it was—no shame to him) representation all the night long, sighing for joy, and filled with unspeakable sweetness. His friend, Giovanni, looking on, had a vision while he stood apart, gazing and wondering at the saint. Giovanni saw, or dreamed, that a beautiful infant—a child dead or in a trance—lay in the manger which he had himself prepared; and that, as Francis bent over the humble bed, the babe slowly awoke, and stretched out its arms towards him. It was the child Christ, dead in the hearts of a careless people, dead or lost in the slumber of a wicked world, but waking up to new life, and kindling the whole slumberous universe around him, at the touch and breath of that supreme love which was in His servant's heart."

S. Francis was remarkable, not only for originating these cribs of Bethany, now seen in every Roman Catholic church throughout the world, and in many a Lutheran Christmas home, but also in being the first to feel the power of his vernacular tongue, and to use it for sacred song. The first rude effort to use Italian for popular hymns and carols was made by S. Francis. His "Song of the Creatures" was the beginning of a national poetry which, sixty years later, reached a climax in the Divine Comedy of Dante. S. Francis set the example—introduced a new power. It was felt at once. There is something as touching in the story of his first introduction to the people of divine psalmody in their own tongue, as there is in the narrative of his institution of the *præsepio*. In an ecstacy he had composed an Italian hymn of praise to God, a sort of Benedicite, in which he calls on all creatures to glorify their Creator. And when he thought it was finished, he heard that a quarrel had broken out in Assisi between the bishop and the magistrates about some petty matter, and the bishop had laid an interdict on the town, and the magistrates, in turn, had outlawed the bishop. S. Francis was deeply affected by this miserable unchristian strife; and finding that it dragged on unhealed, his heart glowed within him, and he added a verse to his hymn :—

> "And praised is my Lord
> By those who, for Thy love, pardon afford,
> And meekly bear the wrongs of men.
> Blessed are those who suffer thus in peace,
> By Thee, the Highest, to be crowned in heaven."

Then " he commanded his disciples to go boldly and seek the great people of the town, and beg them to meet at the bishop's palace." The name of Francis was so potent that it was instantly obeyed. The angry magistrates met in the hall of the indignant bishop in sullen silence, and the few humble Franciscan friars stood between them. Instead of delivering a harangue, a homily from S. Francis, they lifted up their voices, and sang his "Carol of the Creatures." At the sound of the words, in their own Italian tongue, the hearts of bishop and magistrates grew soft; and when the last verse was sung, they rushed into each other's arms, and asked pardon mutually.

Such was the origin of vernacular Italian religious hymns. The companions and disciples of S. Francis continued his work, and their labours have found a modern eloquent historian in M. Ozanam.*

The *præsepio, crèche,* or *krippe,* called forth the first carols. There may have been stray Christmas hymns in the vernacular before, but it was not till the Christmas crib was set up in Minorite chapels, and from thence spread to all Christian churches, that they burst forth throughout the length and breadth of Western Christendom. The representation called for the carol, and the carol, becoming familiar, was sung where there was no crib.†

The Franciscan Manger of the Holy Night assumed another form in the Christmas mysteries, theatrical performances representing the Nativity. These were sometimes performed in churches, but probably not often. At Bayeux, in 1351, Jean de Montdesert, *curé* of S. Malo, in Bayeux, was fined by the Chapter for having had the "Mystery of the Birth of Christ" performed in his church on Christmas Day, 1350. These mysteries contained carols—popular carols—introduced into them to enliven the acting. In the "Mystère de l'Incarnation et Nativité de Notre-Seigneur Jesus Christ," ‡ probably of the year 1474, published by the Brothers Parfait,§ God the

---

\* "Les Poëtes Franciscains."

† In Yorkshire (West Riding) the children still carry about Christmas boxes, lined with coloured paper, in which are figures of the B. Virgin and Child; they sing carols with them, and call them " Milly boxes " (My Lady's box), but have lost all idea of their significance.

‡ Larue : " Essais historiques sur les bardes et jongleurs." Caen, 1834. I., p. 166.

§ Parfait : " Histoire du Théâtre françois." Paris, 1735.

Father orders Gabriel to go to Mary, and announce to her that she is to become the mother of Messiah. Then follows the rubric:—"Adonc chantent le premier vers de la chanson qui suit; et puis les jouers d'instrumens derriere les Anges repetent iceluy vers, et tandis les Anges qui tiennent les instrumens font maniere de jouer. Après les Anges chantent le second vers, et puis les instrumens repetent trois lignes; après les Anges chantent le tiers vers, et puis les instrumens tout le premier et puis la fin." This is the carol:—

"Au nouveau sceu de la Conception
Du Fils de Dieu, pour la Rédemption;
Qui veult faire d'humaine Créatu------re;
Qui estoit cheüe en pé---chié et ordu--re:
Chacun au ciel maine éxul-----tation.
    Faisons grand bruit, chansons multiplions,
    Toutes nos voix ensemble despléons
    Nul ne se faigne, et chacun y ait cure.

TENOR.     Au nouveau sceu.
CONTRA-TENOR.     Au nouveau sceu.
CONCORDANS.     Au nouveau sceu.

"Des instrumens prenons ung million,
En encors plus, bref tout y employon,
Car aujourd'huy a uni sa facture
Avecques soy le hault Dieu de Nature,
Et à tousjours, sans séparation.
    Au nouveau sceu."

When Christ is born the angels again burst out into a carol, with instruments:—

"Au saint naistre du sacré Roy des roys,
Qui de présent est en terre accomply:
Soyons joyeulx, et soit ce lieu rempli
De mélodie, à haulte et clere voix."

And then follows a round, with the refrain, "Loé soit Dieu."

Another mystery of the Nativity, published at Lyons, in 1539, states in its title that it contains carols as well—"Chant Natal contenant sept Noelz, ung Chant Pastoral, et ung Chant Royal, avec ung Mystère de la Nativité, par Personnaiges, composez en imitation verbale, et Musicale de divers Chansons, recüilléz sur l'Escripture Saincte, et d'jcelle illustrez." Whilst Joseph and

Mary are on their way to Bethlehem, they sing a carol, "sur le chant, Le plus souvent tant il m'ennuye."

The annunciation to the shepherds is to the strain of an old Noel—

> "Pasteurs, qui veillez aux champs, (*bis*)
> Oyez mes dicts, et mes chants, (*bis*)
> Je vous annonce la nouvelle
>    Joyeux pour vous :
> Dieu est né --------
>    Pour rachepter tous.
> Allez et l'adorez à genoux."

They go to the stables singing a carol, the refrain of which is "Gloria in excelsis Deo;" and, on reaching it, form round the crib, and sing another on the tune of "Sauvez m'y donc quand vous irez."

> "Chantons Noël, quand nous irons
> Garder nos brebiettes sur l'herbe,
>    Sur l'herbe."

Then David announces on his harp the coming of the Magi, and they arrive and present their gift, each singing an eight-line verse, ending with—

> "Où est-il né, afin que je l'adore?"—

which was the refrain taken up in chorus.

This is a remarkable specimen of a mystery composed out of carols. It contains about 300 lines, and is wholly composed of songs and noels.

Another curious "Comédie de la Nativité de Jésus Christ" was composed by Marguerite de Valois, Queen of Navarre,[*] and it also contains popular carols. Mary and Joseph go to Bethlehem, and search in vain for shelter of three hosts, who refuse them what they ask on different pretexts. One only takes in rich folk, the second only royalty, the third only those who will fiddle and dance. Then Joseph and Mary retire to a stable, and there the Saviour of the world is born. The angels declare His birth to shepherds

---

[*] "Marguerites de la Marguerite des princesses, très-illustre reine de Navarre." Lyons, 1547.

and shepherdesses, who come singing the following carol, with chorus, to the stable:—

SOPHRON & PHILETINA.  Dansons, chantons, faisons rage,
　　　　　　　　　　Puis qu'avons grace pour pardon.
CHORUS.　　　　　　Chantons Noël de bon courage,
　　　　　　　　　　Car nous avons Christ en pardon.

ELPISON & CHRISTELLA.  Saissons Adam, et son lineage,
　　　　　　　　　　Plus avec luy ne demeurons:
　　　　　　　　　　Quitons tous nostre vieil bagage,
　　　　　　　　　　Chevres, Brebis, Chiens, et Moutons;
CHORUS.　　　　　　Chantons Noël, &c.

NEPHALUS & DOROTHEA.  Allons voir Marie la Sage,
　　　　　　　　　　Avec l'enfant de grant renom:
　　　　　　　　　　Dont les Anges en doux langage,
　　　　　　　　　　Nous on fait un si beau sermon.
CHORUS.　　　　　　Chantons Noël, &c.

And so it runs on, sometimes a solo by Dorothea, Christella, Philetina, Sophron, &c., sometimes a duet between shepherd and shepherdess, and the chorus breaking in at intervals.

This singular piece begins, as will be seen, with an invitation to dance as well as sing; and there can be little doubt that some of the carols were sung to a measure accompanied by rhythmic motions of the body, a sort of solemn, sacred dance. S. Ouen, in his life of S. Eligius, couples carols with songs and dances,* but these accompanied "diabolical songs;" the sacred carol was not then known. The name carol is possibly indebted to the same derivative as quadrille and carillon, a song, or dance, or chime, performed by four persons or bells arranged in a square.

The trace of the dance accompanying the carol lingers on to this day. Originally the dance was performed along with profane songs in churches. Religious dances were in vogue among the Romans. They were largely practised also among the Keltic Druids, in honour of Ceridwen. When

---

* "Nullus in festivitate S. Joannis . . . solstitia, aut vallationes, vel saltationes aut Caraulas aut cantica diabolica exerceat." Vit S. Elig., lib. ii. c. 15.

Christianity became the religion of the nations which had practised these religious dances, the Church found great difficulty in suppressing them. Two courses were open to her—either to put them down wholly, or to wash them in pure water, sanctify, and adopt them as drama both to teach and interest the multitude.

In some places she found it necessary to set her face determinedly against them, whilst in other places she tolerated and even sanctioned them.

In 589, the Third Council of Toledo (can. 22) forbade the people dancing through the vigils of saints' days. In 590, the Council of Auxerre forbade *secular* dances in churches (can. 9).* In 858, Gautier, Bishop of Orleans, condemned the rustic songs and female dancers who performed in the Presbytery on Festivals of the Church.

As early as the 9th century, Pope Eugenius II. prohibited dancing and singing base songs in church. Even in 533, the Council of Orleans had forbidden the fulfilment of vows made to sing and dance in churches, "for that such vows anger God, rather than appease Him."

In 1209, the Council of Avignon prohibited theatrical dances and secular songs in churches. In 1212, processions danced round the churches of Paris, and women danced in the cemeteries. In the 17th century, the apprentices and servants of York were accustomed to dance in the nave of the Minster on Shrove Tuesday; and Dean Lake was almost killed by the apprentices for endeavouring to prevent their intrusion into the sacred building for this purpose. There was a curious tenure in Wiltshire, by which the inhabitants of Wishford and Batford went up in a dance annually to Salisbury Cathedral. On Tuesday in Whitsuntide, till the French Revolutionary soldiers destroyed the Cathedral of S. Lambert, at Liège, on that day a deputation of the inhabitants of Verviers danced under the corona in the nave, headed by a cross. The deputation consisted of certain magistrates and clergy of Verviers. To this day, a dancing procession, chanting a curious carol, takes place at Echternach, in Luxemburg, on Tuesday in Whitsun week. It is called the Procession of the Jumping Saints—" Springende Heiligen." It consists of a

---

* "Non licet in Ecclesia choros sæcularium . . . . exercere."

long train of pilgrims, dancing three paces forward and then backward. The pilgrims are headed by the clergy, all dancing. They dance from the bridge over Sauer to the church, round the altar, and separate at the cross in the cemetery. It is to this day a very popular pilgrimage. In 1869, there were 8000 persons in the procession.*

Religious dances are also by no means infrequent in Spain. The following is an account of a Shrove Tuesday performance in the Cathedral at Seville, where it is gone through on that day, on the feast of Corpus Christi, or on that of the Immaculate Conception. The account is from the *Daily Telegraph* of February 22, 1875, and is part of a letter from the special correspondent.

"It was my fortune on Tuesday afternoon behold the performance of an *escuela de baile* of a thoroughly exceptional and of a most surprising nature. I never in my life saw such a sight before; nor, I suppose, am I likely ever to see it again. It was in the Cathedral. The watchful Barlow had warned me that something very curious indeed to view would take place in the great Basilica either a little before or a little after six; and that I was bound even to forego the *table d'hôte* in order to witness it. The sun was setting in the national Spanish colours, bright orange and deep red, as we passed through the noble Moorish gateway—it dates from the twelfth century—called the Puerta del Perdon, and crossing the Patio de las Naranjas, a forecourt full of orange trees hundreds of years old, entered the Cathedral by the portal closest to the Giralda. When from day or even twilight you lift the leathern veil of the doorway and pass into this tremendous fane, you can at first perceive nothing whatsoever. The best thing you can do is to shut your eyes, and allow yourself to be guided onwards for a time. Then lift your eyelids cautiously, and turn your head to either side, and you will begin gradually to discern the enormous columns and the vasty bays around you. By degrees I found that the *trascoro* and the central nave were full of people, nearly all ladies, who were not kneeling, but sitting on the pavement in Oriental fashion, as is customary in Spanish churches when something extraneous to the ordinary ecclesiastical ritual is being performed. Carefully picking my way through the recumbent groups, I came at last within view of the sanctuary and the high altar, which were all ablaze with lights. But there were no celebrants on the altar steps, no acolytes, and not so much as a single minor canon in the stalls, which I thought strange. The *funçion* was evidently not vespers. What was it? Round the great lectern of the *coro*, with its huge illuminated music book, every minim and crotchet as tall as drumsticks, were gathered a dozen of the youngest choristers singing away like so many dying swans. But it was no

---

\* See a full account of it in Krier: "Die Springprocession in Echternach, Luxemb., 1871." For further information on Religious Dances, see an article, by the author of this Introduction, in "The Sacristy," I., p. 63, *seq.*

ordinary chant these children, with their deliciously sweet and clear and silvery voices, sang. It was something quicker, livelier, more jubilant, and, as it seemed to me, more secular than anything I had heard before in a Catholic place of worship, and the singing was accompanied by music quite as gleesome from a band of wind and string instruments. The chant culminated in a ringing exulting pæan of joy; and then, to my utter amazement and bewilderment, the twelve young choristers began to dance round the lectern and before the high altar—absolutely, literally, and operatically to dance. It was the *escuela de baile* without girl performers, and under the highest ecclesiastical auspices. At the close of the proceedings the choristers ranged themselves in line, and a regular and most harmonious fantasia on the castanets was performed. Again, and once again, did the band strike up, and the merry chant, ending with the exulting pæan, was sung, and twice and thrice did the sound of the castanets click through the huge expanse of the mighty Cathedral of Seville. Then I waited to see the little choristers file out of the choir, and down the nave, out of the gate of San Cristobal to their school-house on the other side. They trooped onwards, a demure band of plump, black-eyed, swarthy little fellows, all clad in antique Spanish costume of crimson and yellow doublets and trunk hose, rosettes in their shoes, highly-starched ruffs, and rapiers and plumed hats. Now this spectacle anywhere out of Spain, or, indeed, out of Seville, might have appeared utterly grotesque, unseemly, and indecent. There it appeared quite natural, normal, and in keeping with the surroundings. The castanet dance before the altar was, I was told, a privilege enjoyed solely by the Cathedral of Seville, and was endulged in only thrice a year."

While upon this subject I cannot refrain from quoting two very curious instances of saints leaping for joy in their ecstacy of devotion. One is S. Joseph of Cupertino, an ecstatic Francisan friar, who, one Christmas night, arrayed for Benediction, heard the pfifferari performing Christmas carols outside the church, and at once sprang to the altar, and thence, at one bound, habited in cope, into the pulpit. On another occasion the beautiful hymns made him dance in the middle of the church. The other instance is S. Peter Balsam, who was alone, as he thought, before a statue of the Virgin Mother with the Divine Infant on her knee, and was so overcome by his emotion that he began to dance before it. He was observed by a companion.

The EPIPHANY was also provided with its carols and mysteries, and peculiar dramatical ritual in churches, to impress its significance on the popular mind. The Magi were represented by choristers costumed fantastically, who issued from different corners of the church, as though from different regions of the globe, to meet before the altar. In the Office Book of Rouen, it was ordered that after Terce, the middle king should issue from the east side, the second from the right, the third from the left side of the church. In one of the forms used by the performers, which dates from the 12th century, one of the *dramatis personæ* is an Englishman, and he is thus addressed:—

"Quid stas, quod stupes, bos Britannice?"

to which he replies—"Sto, stupeo, stimulum quæro, ut pugnam bovem Gallicum." * One of the performers was always black—this was Gaspar.† In a sequence of the 16th century we have the following:—

"Gaudete vos fideles, gentium pars electa
Æthiopum nigredo in Judæam est translata."‡

And the carol singers soon followed:—

"Herodes sprach aus grossem Tratz
Ey warumb ist der Hinder so schwarz?
O Lieber Herr er ist uns wohl bekannt
Er is ein König in Morenland."

"Herod spake in great dismay, Why is the hindermost black? O, good Sir, he is well known to us; he is a king of the Moor's country." § To the present day, on the Epiphany at S. Peter's, Rome, at the same moment, three pupils of the Propaganda, of whom one must be a negro, say mass at three altars.

In the rules of the Kremnitz Carol brotherhood, the first king is described as "red," the second as "black," and the third as "green!" ||

Epiphany carols are still sung in Germany and Belgium by men or boys dressed in character. In Holstein three peasants dress in white shirts—one

---

* "Collectanea et Gloses," Beda, Op. iii., 481—Colon. 1688—wrongly attributed to Bede.
† "Jasper erat et ethiops niger, de quo nulli dubium."—John of Hildesheim, p. 13.
‡ Daniel, Hymn v., 180.
§ Docen, Miscel., i., 279.
|| "Schröer in Weim. Jahrsbücher," iii., 408. For much information on representations of the Epiphany, see an article in the "Sacristy," vol. iii., p. 1-18.

has a black face, and carries a fishing-rod with a gilt star suspended to it, and they sing a carol beginning:—

"Wir, Kasper und Melcher, und Baltser genannt,
Wir, sind die heiligen drei König aus Morgenland."

In Saxony the star is composed of oiled paper, and a lamp burns inside it. In the midst of the star a house is painted, and one of the windows is made to open by means of a string, and, like the cuckoo in a clock, a doll of Herod pops out and bobs his head, and then retires again. This exhibition is accompanied by a curious carol, sung in parts, with question and answer, Herod popping out of his window, being supposed to be one of the singers, his part being chanted by the bearer of the star in shrill falsetto. In Hesse three men in white, with blackened faces, sing before each house. At Münstermaifeld, in the Eifel district, a very curious performance takes place. The story of the coming and adoration of the Magi is performed dramatically, the *dramatis personæ* being Herod and his servants, the Jewish Scribes, an angel, two shepherds, and the three kings.

But the most singular performances, those bearing the closest resemblance to the mediæval plays, in which carols were sung in character, is certainly that which prevails in German Bohemia. On the approach of Christmas, boys and girls, dressed as shepherds and sheperdesses, perambulate the towns and villages, singing pastoral songs, the subject of which is the coming of the Christ-child. On the Sundays in Advent, in the Erz mountains, the so-called Angel-host makes its rounds, consisting of two angels, the infant Christ, Bishop Martin of Tours, S. Nicolas or S. Peter, Joseph, Mary, the host of the inn, two shepherds, and the Knecht Ruprecht, a hobgoblin to scare children. At Oberufer, near Pressburg, the parts are carefully prepared in October, with the schoolmaster as instructor, and all the parts are sung, and studied so that they may be sung in good time and tune. No person of disorderly character is allowed to take a character; and whilst the performance lasts, *i.e.* from the first Sunday in Advent to Christmas Eve, no secular music is suffered to be played in the village.

On the first Sunday in Advent the play begins with a procession. First goes the star, carried by the precentor; next the Christmas-tree, hung with ribbands and apples, drawn by the rest of the players, singing sacred songs. On reaching the hall where the miracle play is to be performed, a semi-circle is made, and a carol called the "Star-song" is performed, beginning—

> "Ir lieben meine Singer fangts tapfer an
> Zü grüessen wolln wirs heben an."

The performers then greet the sun, the moon, the stars, the emperor, and the magistracy, "in Namen alles Würz alein soviel als in der Erden, sein" (in the name of all the herbs that grow in earth). They greet next the master-singer and his hat, and conclude with a salutation to the constellations of Charles' wain, the Soul-car of German heathen mythology. After this chanted greeting, with its very heathenish ring, follows a carol, " Unzre eingen sejne bott," whilst singing which the hall is entered.

There is neither stage nor scenery. All the "properties" required are a wooden bench and a straw chair. The bench indicates Bethlehem; the chair, Jerusalem. A choir sings between each scene, and an angel chants the prologue and epilogue. Joseph carries a sort of straw umbrella, which represents the roof of the stable; and the star is affixed to an elongater, like those in toy-boxes on which soldiers are pegged. Knecht Ruprecht, or the Devil, carries a cow's horn and a whip, is dressed in black, and has a hideous mask with horns on his head, and a fox's tail attached to his waist. The three shepherds lie asleep on the floor, and the angel in big boots walks over their breasts, singing, to show that he is communicating his message to them in a dream. The host of the inn wears Hungarian costume, as do also the servants of King Herod—a fur cap, a huzzar coat slung over one shoulder, frogged waistcoats, and hessian boots. The Scribes wear paper frilled collars (like those worn in the reign of Charles I.), paper mitres, white nightshirts, and top boots.[*] It is impossible not to think

---

[*] Engravings of the characters will be found in F. von Reinsberg-Düringsfeld: "Das Festliche Jahr"—Leipzig, 1863, p. 371-7.

of the performance, in *Midsummer Night's Dream*, of Bottom and his company.

In England, Christmas carols have survived; the dancing has been divorced from them, and the personations have disappeared. Epiphany carols have completely died out, and are only now being revived. But, probably, Epiphany was never so popular a festival in England as in Germany. The old miracle plays were often founded on the Apocryphal Gospels; little that is apocryphal has found its way into the carols. There is only one which preserves a trait of myth in it; and that, fortunately, is one of the very highest interest.

I was teaching carols to a party of mill-girls in the West Riding of Yorkshire, some ten years ago, and amongst them that by Dr. Gauntlett—

"Saint Joseph was a walking"—

when they burst out with "Nay! we know one a deal better nor yond;" and, lifting up their voices, they sang, to a curious old strain,—

"Sant Joseph was an old man,
And an old man was he;
He married sweet Mary,
And a Virgin was she.

"And as they were walking
In the garden so green,
She spied some ripe cherries
Hanging over yon treen.*

"Said Mary to Joseph,
With her sweet lips, and smiled,
'Go, pluck me yon ripe cherries off,
For to give to my Child.'

"Said Joseph to the cherry-tree,
'Come, bow to my knee,
And I will pluck thy cherries off,
By one, two, and three.' †

\* \* \* \* \*

---

\* Observe the plural in *n*. † Some verses lost.

> "And as she stooped over Him,
>   She heard angels sing—
> 'God bless our sweet Saviour
>   And our heavenly King.'"  *

Raphael's picture of the Madonna giving cherries to the Child will recur to the mind of the reader.

Hone gives a complete version of the Cherry-Tree Carol—the first verses much like those I heard. There Joseph refuses to pluck the cherries, being minded to put Mary away privily; but he is miraculously informed that the tree will do homage to the pure Mother-Maid:

> "'Go to the tree, Mary,
>   And it shall bow to thee;
> And the highest branch of all
>   Shall bow down to Mary's knee.
>
> "'And she shall gather cherries,
>   By one, by two, by three.'
> 'Now you may see, Joseph,
>   Those cherries were for me.'
>
> "O! eat your cherries, Mary;
>   O! eat your cherries now;
> O! eat your cherries, Mary,
>   That grow on the bough."

This scene occurs in one of the Coventry mystery plays (viii.), when Joseph and Mary are on their way to Bethlehem, before the birth of Christ.

Mary asks,—

> "A very swete husband! wolde ye telle to me
>   What tre is yon, standing upon yon hylle?"
>
> JOSEPH. "For suthe, Mary, it is clepyd a chery tre:
>   In tyme of yer, ye myght ffede you thereon your fylle."
>
> MARY. "Turn ageyn, husband, and behold yon tre,
>   How that it blomyght, now so swetly."

---

* Other versions are given, with other tunes, by Sedding, Sandys, &c.

JOSEPH. "Cum on, Mary, that we wern at yon cyte,
            Or ellys we may be blamyd, I tell you lyhtly."
MARY. "Now, my spouse, I pray you to behold
            How the cheryes growyn upon yon tre;
            Ffor to have them, of reyght, ffayn I wold,
            An it plesyd you to labor' so mec'h for me." *

Joseph answers roughly that he will not stay; then the tree bows down of its own accord, and offers its cherries to the hand of Mary.

There is nothing about the cherry-tree in the Apocryphal Gospels. It is the lingering on of a very curious, mysterious tradition, common to the whole race of man, that the eating of the fruit in Eden was the cause of the descendant of Eve becoming the Mother of Him who was to wipe away that old transgression. In the carol and the mystery play this tradition is strangely altered, but its presence cannot fail to be detected. The following is from the last runa or canto of the "Kalewala," the great Finnish epic, dating from a remote heathen antiquity. It has gone through alteration at the end; the name of the Virgin is given as Mary, and before the Son the old gods of the Suomi are represented as flying to the north:—

"Mariatta, the beautiful maiden, grew up in the lofty mansion; the log of the threshold was stroked by her soft garments, the doorposts by the waving locks of her head.

"Mariatta, the beautiful maiden, always innocent and always pure, went forth to milk the cows.

"Mariatta, the beautiful maiden, always innocent and always pure, went forth to pasture sheep.

"She led them where the serpent glides under the bushes, and where the lizard darts.

"But no serpent glided, no lizard darted, where Mariatta led her sheep.

"On a hill grew a little berry-tree; and it had a green branch, and on the green branch grew a scarlet berry.

"'Come, O virgin!' said the tree, 'come, and gather me.

"'O virgin with the tin broach, come before the worm wounds me, and the black snake has coiled round me.'

"Mariatta, the beautiful maiden, comes forward to pluck the berry, but she cannot reach it. Then she takes a stick and strikes it off, and the berry falls on the ground.

"'Little berry, scarlet berry, come upon my lap.' And the berry danced upon her lap.

"'Little berry, scarlet berry, come up to my lips.' And the berry leaped into her mouth, and she swallowed it."

Mariatta becomes the mother of Ilmori (the Air); and when he is born,

---

* Hone: "Ancient Mysteries" (1823), p. 67-8.

the old Wäinämöinen, the national god of the Finns, "sang his last song, and made a boat of brass, a boat with keel of iron; and in this boat he rowed away, far away into the vast spaces, to the lower regions of the sky." *

The same incident occurs in the "Popol Vuh," the sacred book of the Quiches, a Central American people,† and formed part of the mythology of the ancient Mexicans. The same story has again reappeared from the catacombs of Egypt in the curious romance of the "Two Brothers." ‡ Numerous traces of the same idea may be found, and it might be followed out, and form a most interesting monograph; but this is not the place for such a mythological disquisition. In a note I give a few additional references.§

In conclusion, let us return to S. Francis, with whom we started. Perhaps there is almost as great a need now-a-days of impressing the great doctrine of the Incarnation on the popular mind as in the days of that great regenerator.

The various sects with which England is overrun have more or less Manicheism at their roots. Some of them are lineally traceable to Manicheism in the 8th and 9th centuries. They all more or less sever the spirit from the body, and make religion a matter of spirit only, dissociating from it the body. The sacraments are the outposts of the Incarnation; and with rejection of them, the Incarnation has ceased to be regarded as the keystone of Christianity. Whilst intellectual critics dispute and deny this great verity, its hold on the unintellectual is enfeebled. The great necessity for us at the present day is to enforce this doctrine by every means in our power. We cannot, perhaps, adopt the *præsepio* of S. Francis, but we may his carols. What was found efficacious in the 12th century, will not be

---

\* "Le Kalewala," p. de Lëözan le Duc (1845), ii., 32nd Runa.
† "Popol Vuh," par M. Brasseur de Bourbourg (1861), p. 89 95.
‡ Select Papyri of the British Museum, ii. The best translation is that of M. Maspero, in "Revue des cours littéraires," 1871.
§ Ovid, "Fasti," v., 231, *seq.*; "Arabian Tales," Sequel, by Dom Chaves and M. Cazotte (London, 1798), vol. viii., p. 52; Baltaz. Bonifacio, Hist. Ludicra, Brussels (1656), i., p. 20.

found powerless in the 19th. The carol, in a homely, intelligible manner, brings the doctrine of the Incarnation home to simple minds in a manner which sermons and hymns will never do. It would be well if clergy of the Church of England would adopt the carol, and use it at Christmastide in their churches. They might even attempt the *præsepio* in a schoolroom, and have carols sung around it by their choir. I have assisted at such a performance, in the house of a Calvinist pastor, in the canton of Vaud, and I have seen it attempted with success in the back slums of the East of London in a Church of England school.

S. BARING-GOULD.

EAST MERSEA RECTORY, COLCHESTER,
    *August 5th*, 1875.

# ADVERTISEMENT.

THE use of this book during the holy seasons of Christmas and Epiphany will bring many a new feeling of delight to those who have never yet heard Carols sung in Church. The former series, of which twelve editions were printed, has been adopted on trial since 1868, the first year of publication, in S. Augustine's Church, instead of the hymn book, during the whole of the Christmas and Epiphany seasons; and it is always to us—congregation, choir, and clergy—the very beginning of Lent to lay aside our popular, much-loved carols. "Psalms and Hymns," though appropriate at all other times of joy or sadness, are not the "Spiritual Songs" best suited to express our "great joy" for the "good tidings" of the Saviour's Birth and Manifestation to the Gentiles. The Carol belongs especially to this dispensation. It was introduced by the Angel when he announced the First Christmas; and the Carol has continued the "Evangelical Song" ever since. L'Estrange, in his "Alliance of Divine Offices," cap. 7, p. 211, published A.D. 1690, distinguishes thus :—

"Antiquity called this (the *Gloria in Excelsis*) the Angelical Hymn; and in truth, being *Angelical*, it must be an hymn; αἱ ἄνω δυνάμεις ὑμνοῦσιν οὐ ψάλλουσιν, saith Chrysostom. *Angels and the celestial choir send forth hymns, they sing not psalms*. And so Clemens Alexandrinus—ὕμνοι ἔστων τοῦ Θεοῦ αἱ ᾠδαι—*Let hymns be only the praises of God*; the reason is, οἱ ψαλμοὶ πάντα ἔχουσι, οἱ δὲ ὕμνοι πάλιν οὐδὲν ἀνθρώπινον—*Psalms contain all things both divine and moral, hymns only the praises of God.* Called it is the Angelical Hymn, because the first part thereof is the Nativity Carol (*i.e.* a song or narrative chant sung to a dance or *measure* \*) mentioned by S. Luke, ii. 13, sung by the Angels; the rest was composed by Ecclesiastical Doctors."

Much in the same way Bishop Jeremy Taylor, in his "Life of Christ" part i., sec. iv., 5 and 6, writes:—

"After the Angel had told his message in plain-song, the whole chorus † joined in descant, and sang an hymn to the tune and sense of Heaven, where glory is paid to God in eternal and never-ceasing offices, and whence good-will descends upon men in never-ceasing torrents. Their song was 'Glory be to God,' &c. As soon as these blessed choristers had sung their Christmas carol, and taught the Church a hymn to put into her offices for ever, the Angels returned into Heaven."

Carols have employed the minds and animated the devotion of Christians and poets in all ages and places. They were amongst the first pieces printed by the first printers, a fact which sufficiently indicates their general use. Now, when printing and church music have progressed so far, the true carol ought not to be neglected. With hymns we shall never make Christmas "glad," as in olden time, when the Church in her collect prayed, "God, *which makest us glad* with the yearly remembrance of the birth of Thy Only Son, Jesus Christ, grant that we may with sure confidence behold Him when He shall come to be our Judge." ‡ It might certainly, therefore, tend to regain the love and awaken the homely faith of the masses, if in a more carol-like and free, though at the same time becoming and reverent manner, we

---

\* Baretti, in his Dictionary, explains *carola* to be *ballo tondo che s'accompagna col canto*, a *dance with singing.* "The Scriptures tell us we must *praise the Lord in the dance*," said an old chorister man to me one Christmas night at a choir supper, five-and-twenty years ago, in friend-loving old Cornwall. The remarkable "Flora" dance at Helston just answers to the description in Chaucer's Dreame, "I saw her daunce so comely, carol and sing so sweetly." So in Dante's "Paradise," canto xxiv. 17 v.:—

"Even thus their carols weaving variously
They by the measure paced or swift or slow,
Made me to rate the riches of their joy."

See also *Du Cange's Glossary.*

† Many of the carols in this volume are arranged in like manner—*i.e.* verse, or solo, followed by chorus; and the effect is very striking, and the variation from the ordinary hymn not a little edifying.

‡ Edward VI.'s Prayer Book of 1549, for the first Communion.

were to familiarise, or even popularise, in church and home, this great and fundamental truth of Christianity, the Divine Mystery of the Incarnation. The late Mr. W. Sandys, F.S.A., states that " as the hour of twelve approaches, the carol singers prepare, and the bell-ringers place themselves at their post, to usher in the morning of the Nativity with due rejoicing. The first duty (he says) of a Christian is to repair to his church to return thanks for the benefit conferred on man; he may then with greater satisfaction partake of the subsequent feasting and rejoicing." Telesphorus, in the second century, says in his decretal Epistle—" It is ordained that in the holy night of the Nativity of our Lord and Saviour they do celebrate public church services, and in them do solemnly sing the Angels' hymn." In England, after the Reformation, when Latin hymns were abolished, carols were commonly sung in churches,\* as now in Cornwall, until Epiphany. To assist the further restoration of this pious use of our forefathers, the present enlarged collection is put forth. It is thought to possess, " very considerable merits." If this be so—above all, if even in a small degree it contribute to the heartiness of praise and the loveliness of song—to the Glory, Honour, and Worship of the Divine Jesus—the labours of those who have assisted to bring about this result will have been abundantly rewarded.

The INDEX is not so explicit as it might be; but the thorough-paced people's Carol, such as was sung by vagrant singers, and found in old broadsheet collections and small cheap books printed in the provinces, has scarcely ever author or composer's name handed down. Sometimes the words had a proper tune, sometimes a secular well-known air, and different versions of the same Carol, words and music, were to be found in different counties. In the present work, these versions have undergone careful revision, though it seemed unnecessary to point out either all the alterations, or by whom they were suggested, in this combined effort of many years.

To the following Authors, Publishers, and Owners of Manuscripts, the Rev.

---

\* See Heath's *Account of the Scilly Islands*, quoted by Brand, p. 381; Dr. Goldsmith's *Vicar of Wakefield*, chap. iv.; Warton's notice of *Certain goodly Carowles to be songe to the Glory of God; and Crestenmas Carowles auctorisshed by my lord of London*.

ADVERTISEMENT.

R. R. Chope's grateful thanks are due:—To Mrs. ALEXANDER; to the Rev. Sir HENRY BAKER, Bart., and to the COMPILERS of "Hymns Ancient and Modern;" to the Rev. JOHN BARON; to the Rev. C. BICKNELL; to the Rev. C. J. BLACK; to the Rev. C. T. BOWEN; to Mr. OWEN BREDEN, of S. Mark's College, Chelsea; to the Rev. W. BRIGHT, D.D., Regius Professor of Ecclesiastical History in the University of Oxford; to Mr. ARTHUR HENRY BROWN; to Mrs. O. P. CAMBRIDGE; to the Rev. EDWARD CASWALL; to Mr. JOHN DAVID CHAMBERS; to Mr. WILLIAM CHAPPELL, F.R.S.; to the Rev. S. CHILDS CLARKE; to Mr. NORVAL CLYNE; to WILLIAM TYETH COSTER, M.D.; to M. DE COUSSEMAKER; to the Right Rev. Bishop COXE; to FANNY CROSBY; to the Rev. P. D. DAYMAN; to Mr. W. CHATTERTON DIX; to the Rev. W. D. V. DUNCOMBE, Minor Canon of Hereford Cathedral; to the Rev. J. B. DYKES, Mus. Doc., Vicar of S. Oswald's, Durham; to the Right Rev. the Lord Bishop of Ely, Dr. WOODFORD; to Mrs. C. FAREBROTHER; to Dr. GAUNTLETT; to the Rev. S. BARING-GOULD; to Mr. WILLIAM GOWMAN, a chief player on stringed instruments; to the Rev. GEORGE PEIRCE GRANTHAM; to the Rev. S. S. GREATHEED; to the Proprietor of the "Guardian;" to the Rev. ARCHER GURNEY; to Mr. JAMES HALSE, a chief player on stringed instruments; to the Rev. R. S. HAWKER, Vicar of Morwenstow; to the Rev. THOMAS HELMORE, Priest-in-Ordinary to the Queen, &c.; to Mr. JOHN HODGES; to Mr. W. R. HOLT; to the Rev. WILLIAM JOSIAH IRONS, D.D., Prebendary of S. Paul's, &c.; to Miss GENEVIÈVE IRONS; to Mr. HERBERT STEPHEN IRONS, Assistant Organist of Chester Cathedral; to the Right Rev. Bishop JENNER; to J. E. B.; to Mr. DAVID JONES, for much help in collecting local Carols, as well as for search made in the British Museum; to the Society for Promoting Christian Knowledge; to Mr. HENRY LAHEE; to the Rev. W. LAYING; to the Rev. F. G. LEE, D.C.L.; to the Right Rev. the Lord Bishop of Lincoln, Dr. CHRISTOPHER WORDSWORTH; to Mr. GEORGE B. LISSANT, Organist of S. Augustine's Church, South Kensington; to the Rev. R. F. LITTLEDALE, LL.D.; to Messrs. SAMPSON LOW, SON, and MARSTON; to Messrs. MASTERS and Co.; to Messrs. METZLER and Co; to the Rev. J. E. MILLARD, D.D.; to Mr. MOON; to the Rev. A. M. MORGAN; to the Rev. GERARD MOULTRIE; to Messrs. NOVELLO, EWER, and Co.; to Mr. H. J. PEEL; to P. V.; to Dr. RIMBAULT, to whom the Church is largely indebted for antiquarian research; to Mr. W. SANDYS; to Mr. E. SEDDING; to the Rev. H. FLEETWOOD SHEPPARD; to the Rev. R. F. SMITH, Minor Canon of Southwell Collegiate Church; to Mr. SAMUEL SMITH, Organist of S. John's, Windsor; to Dr. STAINER, Organist of S. Paul's Cathedral; to Mr. WILLIAM THORNE; to the Rev. GODFRLY THRING; to Messrs. WEEKES and Co.; and to Mr. GEORGE S. WEEKES.

R. R. C.

# INDEX.

*The Words and Music, marked thus \*, are Copyright of the Rev. R. R. Chope, as well as many of the other Harmonies and altered Words of Traditional Carols.*

| FIRST LINE OF CAROL. | NO. | AUTHOR OR SOURCE OF WORDS. | MUSIC. |
|---|---|---|---|
| All hail the star in Judah's sky | 87 | Rev. W. J. Irons, D.D. | From William Gowman |

This work would not have reached its present state of poetic beauty and doctrinal accuracy of expression without the valuable help of my esteemed friend, Dr. Irons.

| | | | |
|---|---|---|---|
| All shall call thee blessed | 110 | Rev. W. J. Irons, D.D. | George B. Lissant' |
| Angel hosts in bright array | 65 | Rev. Geo. Peirce Grantham | From William Gowman* |

Had it not been for the persevering, though unobtrusive, labours of Mr. William Gowman, many of these beautiful melodies must have been lost to the services of the Church.

| | | | |
|---|---|---|---|
| Angels, from the realms of glory | 3 | . . . . | Herbert Stephen Irons |

This copyright tune is taken from the Rev. R. R. Chope's "Hymn and Tune Book," published by Mr. Mackenzie.

| | | | |
|---|---|---|---|
| Arouse thee, Herod, fling | 104 | Rev. Geo. Peirce Grantham | Rev. R. F. Smith* |

If any inquire what the clergy of this generation have done for the sacred service of song in the Church of Christ, they may form a fair estimate of their successful labours from the compositions in this work.

| | | | |
|---|---|---|---|
| A shout of mighty triumph | 54 | Rev. Geo. Peirce Grantham | 1 Rev. R. F. Smith*<br>2 Rev. G. P. Grantham* |
| As Joseph was a walking | 26 | H. J. Gauntlett | H. J. Gauntlett, Mus. Doc. 1849 |
| As on the night before this happy morn | 42 | George Wither | Orlando Gibbons |

This carol is from the "Hymns and Songs of the Church," translated and composed by George Wither, and printed by his "Assignes," A.D. 1623. "Master Orlando Gibbons" supplied no music for the chorus. My friend, Mr. H. S. Irons, who has a true smack of good old Church music in him, has carefully remedied the defect. His arrangements throughout this book will be found to possess considerable merit, and demand some skill in the accompanist.

| | | | |
|---|---|---|---|
| As with gladness men of old | 101 | W. Chatterton Dix | Rev. R. F. Smith* |

This beautiful carol had been so much associated with hymn music, that it was no easy matter to get disentangled from the style; but my skilful friend, who has a true conception of carol music, successfully effected this for me at last. I ought here to acknowledge how much I am indebted to the Rev. R. F. Smith for his painstaking zeal and ability in suggesting alterations and improvements in the proofs submitted to him of both music and words.

| | | | |
|---|---|---|---|
| A Virgin most pure, as the prophets do tell | 21 | Traditional, altered | Traditional, W. of England |

This arrangement of a deservedly popular old carol goes splendidly.

| | | | |
|---|---|---|---|
| *Be hushed, ye earth and silver skies | 62 | Rev Geo. Peirce Grantham | Rev. Geo. Peirce Grantham* |
| Be present, ye faithful | 25 | Translated from the Latin | Arranged by Herbert Stephen Irons |

xxx                                    INDEX.

*The Words and Music, marked thus *, are Copyright of the Rev. R. R. Chope, as well as many of the other Harmonies and altered Words of Traditional Carols.*

|  |  | AUTHOR OR SOURCE OF |  |
|---|---|---|---|
| FIRST LINE OF CAROL. | NO. | WORDS. | MUSIC. |
| Blithely from the mouldering church-yard | 14 | J. E. B. | Rev. R. F. Smith* |

The words of this carol were first published in the *Guardian*.

| Bright Angel hosts are heard on high | 30 | Cornish, altered by R.R.C. | Cornish |
| Brightest and best of the sons of the morning | 99 | Bishop Heber | Herbert Stephen Irons* |
| Calm on the listening ear of night | 40 | Edmund Hamilton Sears | Devonshire |
| Carol, carol, Christians | 46 | Bishop Coxe | Rev. R. F. Smith* |

In the early ages bishops were accustomed to sing carols among the clergy. Bishop Aldhelm sang sacred songs to his harp on bridges and in thoroughfares. See Churton's *Early English Church*, c. vii., pp. 133, 134. Also Brand's *Popular Antiquities*, vol. i., p. 480. And for some account of music in the Anglo-Saxon Church, Johnson's *English Canons* (Oxford, 1850), Preface, pp. xvi., xvii., Notes.

| Carol, sweetly carol | 47 | Fanny Crosby | P. V. |

Inserted with the kind permission of Messrs. Weekes & Co.

| Christians, awake, salute the happy morn | 32 | John Byrom | R. Wainwright, Mus. Doc. |
| Christians, carol sweetly | 13 | William Chatterton Dix | Herbert Stephen Irons* |
| Come, good Christians, join our song | 84 | Rev. S. Baring-Gould | French Flanders, harmonised by H. S. I. |

The end of the 16th or the beginning of the 17th century appears to be the date of this music, which is very interesting, as containing most unmistakably the "motif" of the latter part of Handel's well-known "Harmonious Blacksmith." The words, slightly altered, and music are inserted here with the kind permission of Mr. John Hodges.

| Come! ye lofty, come! ye lowly | 60 | Rev. Archer Gurney | Rev. Archer Gurney |
| Deep the gloom, and still the night | 81 | Rev. G. P. Grantham | Rev. G. P. Grantham |

This popular carol (inserted with the kind permission of Mr. John Hodges) was sung at Christmas in the Free Trade Hall, Manchester, by 300 voices, under the direction of the Rev. Thomas Helmore, and before 4000 persons, "with thunders of applause."

| *Earnest-hearted Soul, O why | 109 | Rev. R. F. Smith | Rev. R. F. Smith* |
| Fearfully, timidly, now do we raise | 102 | Slightly altered by R. F. S. | H. J. Gauntlett, Mus. Doc. |

Give the accented syllable to the accented note, and everything falls into its proper place in this carol.

| From the Eastern mountains | 86 | Rev. Godfrey Thring | George B. Lissant* |
| Gentle Saviour, day and night | 78 | Tr. by Rev. S. Baring-Gould | French Flanders, harmonised by the Rev. H. Fleetwood Sheppard |

This is another of the Flemish Noels—one of the stock pieces of the carol singers of Dunkerque; but it is also known and sung in other parts of the country. It is inserted here with the kind permission of Mr. John Hodges.

| Gently falls the winter snow | 19 | Rev. E. Caswall & W. J. I. | Herbert Stephen Irons* |

# INDEX. xxxi

*The Words and Music, marked thus\*, are Copyright of the Rev. R. R. Chope, as well as many of the other Harmonies and altered Words of Traditional Carols.*

| FIRST LINE OF CAROL. | NO. | AUTHOR OR SOURCE OF WORDS. | MUSIC. |
|---|---|---|---|
| Glory to God in the highest is ringing | 16 | Rev. W. J. Irons, D.D. | Rev. R. F. Smith\* |

Striking music to striking words. Hand-bells or stringed instruments would be effective as additional accompaniments. The "Nowells" of this bell-carol should not be sung when they can be played on an organ or other instrument.

| | | | |
|---|---|---|---|
| God rest you, merry gentlemen | 10 | 1 Traditional | 1 Arranged by the Rev. W. D. V. Duncombe |
| | | 2 Traditional, altered | 2 Arranged by Herbert Stephen Irons |

There are two or three varieties of this carol in the minor, and one in the major key. The form No. 1 here given is believed to be the truly national one—the least corrupt, and the best. Certainly the harmonies are good, and will stand no end of wear. The true carol must not be made up of inferior harmonies. There should be an undeniably melodious flow of the middle parts, as a general rule. N.B.—The last chord in the last verse of No. 1 should be sung with the A♯. No carol seems to be more generally known than this.

| | | | |
|---|---|---|---|
| God's dear Son without beginning | 5 | From Gilbert's Book | West of England, arranged by Rev. W. D. V. Duncombe |
| Good Christians all, with sweet accord | 22 | Re-written by R. R. C. | Cornish |
| Hark! all around the welkin rings | 61 | British Museum | Owen Breden |
| Hark, hark, what news the Angels bring | 18 | Devonshire, altered by R. R. C. | Devonshire, altered by Herbert Stephen Irons |
| \*Hark! the full-voiced choir is singing | 38 | Rev. R. R. Chope | From William Gowman, arranged by Herbert Stephen Irons\* |
| Hark! the herald Angels sing | 17 | Rev. Charles Wesley | F. Mendelssohn Bartholdy |
| Hark! the music of the Cherubs | 31 | Cornish, and R. R. C. | Traditional, arranged by Herbert Stephen Irons\* |

These carols should be well practised before they are played in the Services of the Church.

| | | | |
|---|---|---|---|
| Hark! what mean those holy voices | 41 | Traditional | Cornish |

It was a custom in Cornwall to repeat each verse of some carols to the second part of the music, as in this specimen.

| | | | |
|---|---|---|---|
| Hark! what mean those thrilling voices | 63 | Altered from Cawood by H. J. Gauntlett and R. R. C. | H. J. Gauntlett, Mus. Doc. 1867 |

The music is in the time of the Church March, and form of the Church Dance.

| | | | |
|---|---|---|---|
| High let us swell our tuneful notes | 37 | From the end of the Prayer Book | Henry Lahee |
| How blest with more than woman's bliss was she | 88 | Traditional, and W. J. I. | From James Halse, arranged by Herbert Stephen Irons\* |
| \*I love to hear sweet voices sing | 23 | Rev. R. R. Chope | From William Gowman, arranged by Herbert Stephen Irons\* |

The sweet memory of carols sung at midnight on Christmas Eve suggested these lines to their author.

# INDEX.

*The Words and Music, marked thus\*, are Copyright of the Rev. R. R. Chope, as well as many of the other Harmonies and altered Words of Traditional Carols.*

| FIRST LINE OF CAROL. | NO. | AUTHOR OR SOURCE OF WORDS. | MUSIC. |
|---|---|---|---|
| Immortal Babe, who this dear day | 50 | Bishop Hall | Rev. R. F. Smith\* |

The words of this beautiful carol were written for the Exeter Cathedral Choir.

| | | | |
|---|---|---|---|
| I sing the birth was born to-night. | 12 | Ben Johnson, A.D. 1600 | Rev. R. F. Smith\* |

The mixture of major and minor in this carol is greatly appreciable.

| | | | |
|---|---|---|---|
| It came upon the midnight clear. | 34 | Edmund Hamilton Sears. | Samuel Smith\* |
| \*Knowing not the great Creator. | 100 | Literal translation by Rev. S. Baring-Gould | Katholische Gesangbuch, Dresden, 1767, harmonised by R. F. S. |

This charming little Epiphany carol is taken from the Trèves book of Ecclesiastical music.

| | | | |
|---|---|---|---|
| Last night I lay me down to sleep. | 36 | Rev. J. E. Millard, D.D. | Herbert Stephen Irons\* |

This carol embraces the old religious belief that a guardian angel presides over each bed.

| | | | |
|---|---|---|---|
| Let Christians all with one accord rejoice | 82 | Traditional | Arthur Henry Brown\* |
| Let heaven and earth rejoice and sing | 9 | Traditional | Traditional Cornish |
| \*Let us now go to Bethlehem | 27 | Rev. R. R. Chope | Old English, arranged by Herbert Stephen Irons |
| Like silver lamps in a distant shrine | 43 | William Chatterton Dix | George B. Lissant\* |

"Excellent and original" music, set to truly poetical words.

| | | | |
|---|---|---|---|
| Listen, Gentles, to the story | 55 | Tr. by Rev. S. Baring-Gould | Flemish from Coussemaker's book, harmonised by the Rev. H. Fleetwood Sheppard |

This carol, inserted with the kind permission of Mr. John Hodges, is very pleasing when sung quick enough. It belongs to the early part of the last century. The text, in the original, is somewhat fragmentary; it is, in fact, being fast forgotten.

| | | | |
|---|---|---|---|
| Look, shepherds, look! Why? Where? | 53 | From the Ashmolean Museum, modernised by R. R. C. | Herbert Stephen Irons\* |
| Look up to heaven, lo! stars are there | 90 | Rev. W. J. Irons, D.D. | Rev. R. F. Smith\* |

The words were written expressly for this work.

| | | | |
|---|---|---|---|
| Lord, with what zeal did Thy first martyr | 70 | George Wither. | Orlando Gibbons, arranged by H. S. I. |
| Lo! the pilgrim Magi. | 79 | John David Chambers, from the Latin | Herbert Stephen Irons\* |

This carol is written to be sung in procession, and it is very good.

| | | | |
|---|---|---|---|
| Lo! unto us a Child is born. | 49 | Traditional, and R. R. C. | Cornish |

This is a delightful carol, of the true Cornish style of music.

| | | | |
|---|---|---|---|
| \*Noel. Born is the King of Israel. | 96 | Rev. W. J. Irons, D.D. | Arthur Henry Brown\* |

The music of this carol was first published in the *Choir*, by Messrs. Metzler & Co.

# INDEX.

xxxiii.

*The Words and Music, marked thus \*, are Copyright of the Rev. R. R. Chope, as well as many of the other Harmonies and altered Words of Traditional Carols.*

| FIRST LINE OF CAROL. | NO. | WORDS. (AUTHOR OR SOURCE OF) | MUSIC. |
|---|---|---|---|
| Noel. This is the salutation of the angel Gabriel. | 45 | Last two verses by the Rev. R. R. Chope | Old English |
| Now lift the carol, men and maids. | 7 | Rev. A. M. Morgan | Arthur Henry Brown* |

The music of this carol is the author's special favourite.

| | | | |
|---|---|---|---|
| *O ! come ye down to Cana. | 106 | Rev. G. P. Grantham | H. J. Gauntlett, Mus. Doc. 1874 |
| O lovely voices of the sky | 92 | Mrs. Hemans | Traditional, arranged by Herbert Stephen Irons |

In Mr. William Sandy's admirable book of "Christmas Carols, Ancient and Modern," this beautiful melody is set to the words, "Saint Stephen was an holy man"—a kind of narrative in verse of the account recorded in the Acts of the holy Apostles, but too quaint in style for use in church.

| | | | |
|---|---|---|---|
| Once again, O blessed time. | 39 | Rev. William Bright, D.D. | Rev. J. B. Dykes, Mus. Doc. |

From "Carols, New and Old," by the Rev. H. Bramley and Dr. Stainer, with the kind permission of Messrs. Novello, Ewer & Co.

| | | | |
|---|---|---|---|
| Once in royal David's city | 58 | Mrs. Alexander | H. J. Gauntlett, Mus. Doc. 1856. |
| Once in the winter cold, when earth | 66 | Rev. C. J. Black | Rev. R. F. Smith* |
| *O sing of the Saviour's might | 108 | Rev. R. R. Chope | Samuel Smith* |

This effective tune was taken down from some carollers in the village of Marden, in Herefordshire, in which county a laudable effort has been made to restore carol singing.

| | | | |
|---|---|---|---|
| *O sing we a carol all blithe and free | 24 | Rev. W. J. Irons, D.D. | Arthur Henry Brown* |

These telling words were expressly written for Mr. Brown's admirable carol.

| | | | |
|---|---|---|---|
| *Remember, life is short, O man. | 76 | Re-written for R. R. C. by the Rev. W. J. Irons, D.D. | Traditional, arranged by Herbert Stephen Irons |

It was formerly believed that this piece contained the original of *God save the King*.

| | | | |
|---|---|---|---|
| Rise, wondering shepherds, rise | 51 | Traditional, Devonshire | Arranged by Herbert Stephen Irons* |

The duet parts of this carol must be sung *without* accompaniment, or much of the effect will be lost.

| | | | |
|---|---|---|---|
| Shepherds, rejoice, lift up your eyes | 35 | Traditional, W. of England | Traditional, harmonised by H. S. I. |

The inner parts of many of these carols are strikingly beautiful and melodious.

| | | | |
|---|---|---|---|
| *Shining o'er Bethlehem, to faithful watchers given | 103 | Rev. R. F. Smith | Old English, arranged by Herbert Stephen Irons |

This air is taken from Mr. William Chappell's admirable book of "Popular Music of the Olden Time."

| | | | |
|---|---|---|---|
| *Sing we merry Christmas | 1 | Rev. C. T. Bowen | Rev. C. T. Bowen* |
| *Sing ye the songs of praise. | 57 | Rev. W. Layng | Mrs. C. Farebrother* |
| Sleep, holy Babe. | 75 | Rev. E. Caswall | Orlando Gibbons, and H. S. Irons* |
| *Sleep, my Saviour, sleep | 74 | Rev. S. Baring-Gould | Bohemian, arranged by Rev. R. F. Smith* |
| Sojourners and strangers | 107 | Rev. W. J. Irons, D.D. | Herbert Stephen Irons* |

c

## INDEX.

*The Words and Music, marked thus \*, are Copyright of the Rev. R. R. Chope, as well as many of the other Harmonies and altered Words of Traditional Carols.*

| FIRST LINE OF CAROL. | NO. | WORDS. | MUSIC. |
|---|---|---|---|
| Songs of thankfulness and praise. | 85 | Bishop of Lincoln (Christopher Wordsworth, D.D.) | George B. Lissant* |
| Star of heaven, new glory beaming | 83 | Rev. W. J. Irons, D.D. | John Stainer, M.A., Mus. Doc.* |

This is one of many excellent carols now set to music for the first time.

| | | | |
|---|---|---|---|
| *Stars all bright are beaming | 4 | Rev. R. R. Chope | Mr. Moon and W. R. Holt |

A great favourite in the congregation.

| | | | |
|---|---|---|---|
| Teach us by his example, Lord | 71 | George Wither. | From William Gowman |
| That rage whereof the Psalm doth say | 72 | George Wither. | Rev. R. F. Smith* |
| That so Thy blessed birth, O Christ | 94 | George Wither. | Orlando Gibbons |
| The Babe in Bethlehem's manger laid | 6 | Kentish | Traditional |

The Compiler's object has been to include in this collection every English carol worth preserving, and capable of being still used in the services of the church.

| | | | |
|---|---|---|---|
| The blasts of chill December sound | 64 | Norval Clyne | Rev. R. F. Smith* |
| The cedar of Lebanon, plant of renown | 11 | Rev. R. F. Littledale, LL.D. | Old English |
| *The Christmas bells are ringing. | 67 | Rev. G. P. Grantham | Flemish, arranged by Herbert Stephen Irons* |
| The first Noel that the Angel did say | 80 | Traditional, emended | Traditional |
| *The flocks were wrapt in slumber all along the dewy ground | 29 | Rev. R. F. Smith | Rev R. F. Smith* |

Certainly this is a king of carols—grand, flowing, melodious; full of life but majestic and dignified withal.

| | | | |
|---|---|---|---|
| The holly and the ivy. | 15 | Traditional | Old French |

"Dear Aunt Mary's tree," to quote the Cornish poet, has been looked upon from time immemorial as emblematic of the Saviour's mission.

| | | | |
|---|---|---|---|
| *The King of kings | 105 | Miss Geneviève Irons | Rev R. F. Smith* |
| The Lord at first did Adam make. | 2 | West of England, emended | From Gilbert's book |

This carol is taken from Davies Gilbert's "Ancient Christmas Carols, with the Tunes to which they were formerly sung in the West of England," first published in 1822. They were sung, he says, in churches and in private houses at Christmas up to the latter part of the late century; but the writer of this himself joined in singing carols in the churches of the West as recently as twenty years before he so successfully introduced them to his own congregation in London.
Christmas Day, like other great Festivals, has a Vigil, or Fast. The Holy Eucharist is celebrated at midnight after Christmas Eve, when austerities cease, and rejoicings begin, and the peculiarly appropriate carol succeeds to the "Advent cry."

| | | | |
|---|---|---|---|
| The Lord is come | 91 | Traditional | Cornish |
| The moon shone bright, and the stars gave light | 77 | Traditional | Traditional, Lancashire. |

From "Carols, New and Old," with the kind permission of Messrs. Novello, Ewer & Co. The last verse should be omitted when this carol is sung in church.

| | | | |
|---|---|---|---|
| The snow lay deep upon the ground | 44 | Traditional | West of England |

INDEX. XXXV

*The Words and Music, marked thus* *, are Copyright of the Rev. R. R. Chope, as well as many of the other Harmonies and altered Words of Traditional Carols.*

| FIRST LINE OF CAROL. | NO. | WORDS. | AUTHOR OR SOURCE OF MUSIC. |
|---|---|---|---|
| The Son of God goes forth to war. | 69 | Bishop Heber . . . | Rev. R. F. Smith* |

Much of the effect of this clever carol depends on the pace at which is sung. It is written as a *Processional*. The time is either $\frac{6}{4}$ or $\frac{12}{8}$; two steps should be taken to the bar in the quick parts, and four in the slow.

| The winter sun was setting. . | 73 | Rev. G Peirce Grantham . | 1. French, arranged by the Rev. W. D. V. Duncombe. 2. Rev. Thomas Helmore* |

In the second tune the first syllable, "with," "both," "till," of the seventh line of verses 2, 3, 4, should be sung as a crotchet.

| *The wise men saw a light afar . | 28 | Rev. R. R. Chope . | H. J. Gauntlett, Mus. Doc. 1849. |

This music is abbreviated from Dr. Gauntlett's carol of "The Three Ships," or, "The Saviour Christ and our Ladye," 1849.

| The Word made flesh, right reverently . . . . | 56 | Tr. by Rev. S. Baring-Gould | Latin sequence, harmonised by Rev. H. Fleetwood Sheppard |

The version of the melody here chosen is from the Amiens collection of liturgical music. It is quite a gem, and the arrangement admirably congruous. This reprint is from the "Sacristy," with the kind permission of Mr. John Hodges.

| *There came three kings, ere break of day . . . . . | 95 | Rev. Gerald Moultrie . | Rev. R. F. Smith* |
| There were shepherds abiding in the field . . . . | 52 | S. Luke ii. ver. 8 . | Partly traditional, partly Herbert Stephen Irons* |
| *This day a Child is born . . | 8 | Rev. R. R. Chope . | Traditional |
| Thou art our God, we exalt Thee, we praise Thee . . . | 93 | Rev. W. J. Irons, D.D. . | Herbert Stephen Irons* |

This is an especial favourite of the poor.

| To earth from heaven glad tidings I unfold. . . . . | 89 | John David Chambers, from the Latin . | Herbert Stephen Irons* |
| Upon the snow-clad earth without. | 59 | Slightly altered by R. R. C. | H. J. Gauntlett, Mus. Doc. 1856 |
| Welcome that star in Judah's sky. | 93 | Rev. Rbt. Stephen Hawker | Herbert Stephen Irons* |

Here is a beautiful carol by one of Cornwall's greatest poets—a true son of the Church—a faithful friend of the revered Henry Philpotts, Bishop of Exeter, whose light, set on a hill, could not be hid. For upwards of forty years Robert Stephen Hawker was Vicar of Morwenstow; and, though his last moments were spent in the great town by the Tamar's mouth, his last conscious thoughts and feeble steps were bent in the direction of his sea-girt home among the wild cliffs of Morwenstow.

| What Child is this, who, laid to rest | 48 | William Chatterton Dix | Traditional |
| *What joy for Mary, blessed Maid. | 111 | Rev. W. J. Irons, D.D. | Arthur Henry Brown* |

Numeral carols were common in the olden time. The ancient Hebrew is very curious. With each number the previous numbers are repeated, so that each verse includes all the previous, like a well-known nursery carol, until at last we have the summing up—"Who knows thirteen? I know thirteen; thirteen divine emanations; twelve tribes; eleven stars (cf. Gen. xxxvi 9); ten commandments, nine months of gestation; eight days of circumcision; seven days of the week; six books of Mishneh; five books of the Law; four holy matrons (viz., Sarah, Rebecca, Leah, Rachel); three patriarchs; two tables of the Covenant; One is our God, Who is over heaven and earth." But it is impossible to insert in any book for use in church the "Seven Joys" or the "New Dial." The words and music here given are worthy substitutes.

c 2

*The Words and Music, marked thus \*, are Copyright of the Rev. R. R. Chope, as well as many of the other harmonies and altered Words of Traditional Carols.*

| FIRST LINE OF CAROL. | NO. | WORDS. | MUSIC. |
|---|---|---|---|
| What notes shall suit the song divine | 33 | J. Waring | Arranged by Herbert Stephen Irons* |
| When Christ was born of pure Marie | 97 | Traditional, altered by Rev. R. R. Chope | Herbert Stephen Irons* |

The original words are preserved in an old MS. of the Harleian collection in the British Museum.

| | | | |
|---|---|---|---|
| *When the crimson sun had set | 68 | Rev. Geo. Peirce Grantham | Traditional, arranged by the Rev. S. S. Greatheed* |
| While shepherds watched their flocks by night | 20 | Nahum Tate | From William Gowman, arranged by Herbert Stephen Irons* |
| Who is this from Bethlehem coming | 112 | Rev. W. J. Irons, D.D. | Herbert Stephen Irons* |

This carol is composed partly in the ancient, partly in the modern style of music.

R. R. CHOPE.

*Wilton House, Hereford Square, S.W.,* 1875.

# Christmas Eve.

**Carol 1.**

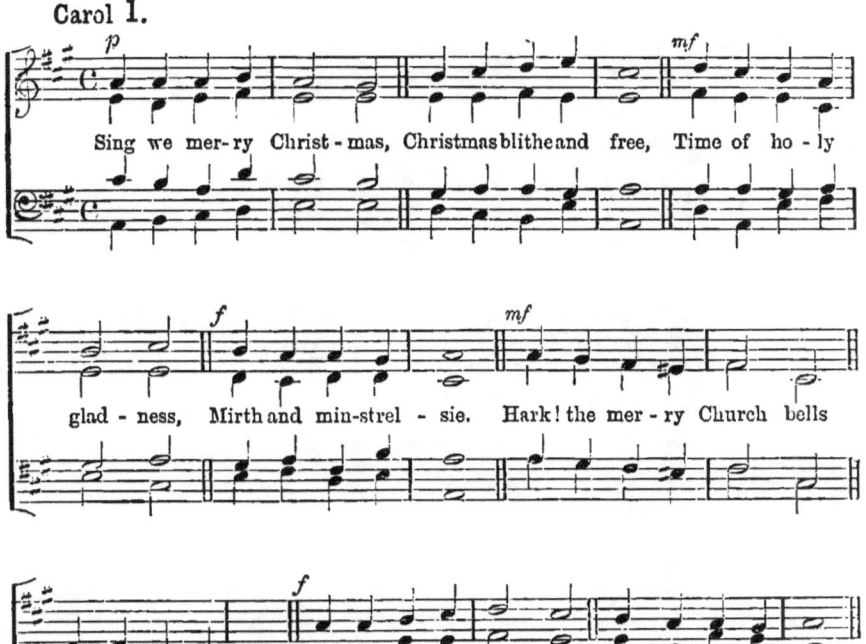

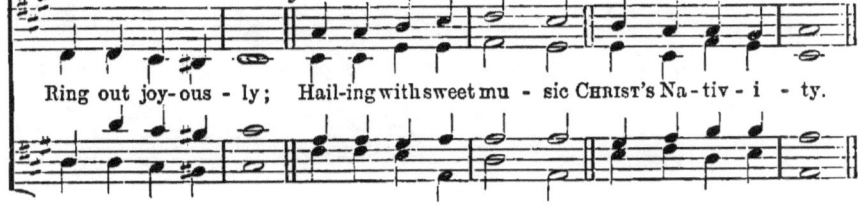

*mf* Haste we to His Temple,
　　Wreathe our garlands green,
　　Deck each arch and column,
　　Stall and Altar Screen.
*f* Gloria in excelsis;
　　Hark! the Angels sing!
　　Gloria in supremis,
　　To our Infant KING.

*f* Priest, and choir, and people,
　　Join in concert all,
　　Sing your loudest praises,
　　At our Festival.
*mf* Joy for us poor exiles,
　　Dawns this happy Morn,—
*ff* JESUS CHRIST, the SAVIOUR,
　　Unto us is born!

# Christmas Eve.

**Carol 2.**

*mf* And thus within the garden he
    Commanded was to stay ;
    And unto him for statute good
    These words the LORD did say :
    " The fruit that in the garden grows
    To thee shall be for meat,
    Except the tree in midst thereof,
    Of which thou shalt not eat."
        Now let good Christians, &c.

"For in the day that thou dost touch,
    Or unto it come nigh,—
    Or if that thou should'st eat thereof,
*p*   Then thou shalt surely die."
*mf* But Adam he did take no heed
    To that same only thing,
*dim* But did transgress GOD's holy Laws,
    And sore was wrapp'd in sin.
    *mf*  Now let good Christians, &c.

*mf* Now mark the Goodness of the LORD,
    Which He to mankind bore ;
    His Mercy soon He did extend,
    Lost man for to restore ;
*cr* And then, for to redeem our souls
    From death, and hell, and thrall,
*dim* He said His Own dear SON should come,
    The SAVIOUR of us all.
    *mf*  Now let good Christians, &c.

And now the Tide is nigh at hand,
    In which our SAVIOUR came ;
*cr* Let us rejoice and merry be,
    In keeping of the same.
*f*  Let's feed the poor and clothe the bare,
    And love both great and small,
*dim* That when we die, to Heaven at last
    Our LORD may bring us all.
    *mf*  Now let good Christians, &c.

# Christmas Eve.

Carol 3.

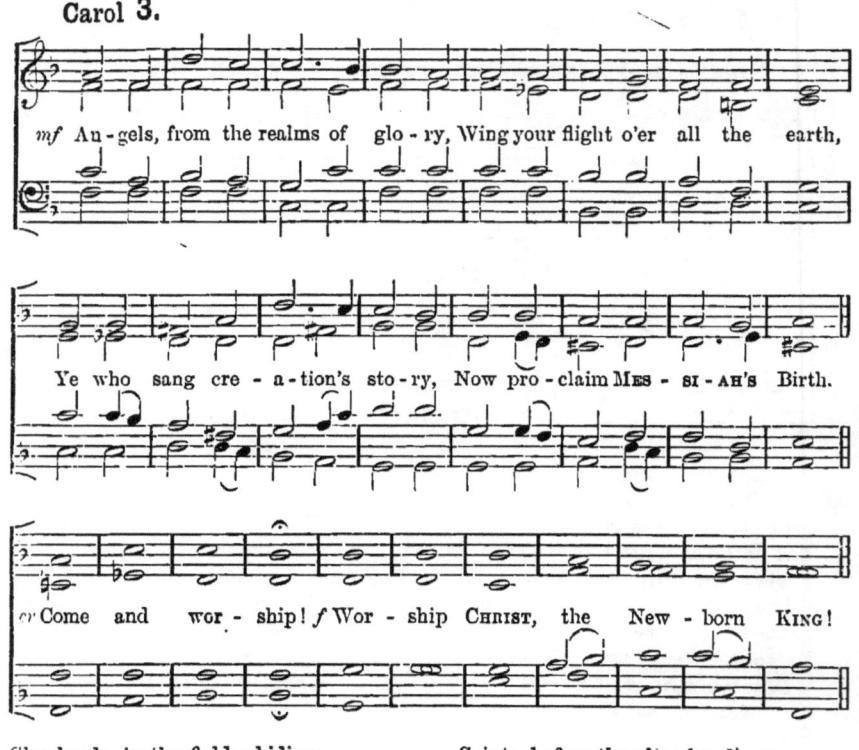

*mf* Angels, from the realms of glory, Wing your flight o'er all the earth,
Ye who sang creation's story, Now proclaim MESSIAH's Birth.
*cr* Come and worship! *f* Worship CHRIST, the New-born KING!

  *p* Shepherds, in the fields abiding,
     Watching o'er your flocks by night,
  God with man is now residing,
*mf*    Yonder shines the Heavenly Light:
*cr*       Come and worship!
*f*    Worship CHRIST, the New-born KING!

  Saints, before the altar bending,
     Watching long in hope and fear;
*mf* Suddenly the LORD, descending,
     In His Temple shall appear.
*cr*     Come and worship!
*f*    Worship CHRIST, the New-born KING!

  Saints and Angels join in praising
    Thee, the FATHER, SPIRIT, SON,
  Evermore their voices raising
    To the Eternal THREE IN ONE;
*cr*     Come and worship!
*ff*    Worship CHRIST, the New-born KING!

# Christmas Carols.

**Carol 4.**

*mf* Stars all bright are beam-ing From the skies a-bove, Na-ture's face all gleam-ing, Shines with Heaven's own love. *f* Wake and sing, good Christ-ians, On this Birth-day Morn, Heaven and earth are tell-ing God for man is born.

*p* Here for us abiding,
　Cradled in a Stall,
All His glory hiding,
　See the Lord of all!
　　*f* Wake and sing, &c.

*mf* Born that He might lead us
　From this desert home,—
Guide our way, and feed us,
　Till the end shall come!
　　*f* Wake and sing, &c.

*f* Thousand thousand blessings
　Sing we for His Love,
Choral Hymns addressing
　To our Lord above.
　　Wake and sing, &c.

*f* Glory in the Highest,
　For this wondrous Birth;
Choir of Heaven! thou criest
*pp*　Peace to all the earth!
　　*ff* Wake and sing, &c.

# Christmas Carols.

Carol 5.

do us good, With ma-ny a pur-ple bleed-ing wound.

*mf* Bethlehem, King David's city,
  Was His Birthplace, as we find,—
  Who GOD and MAN endued with pity
  Was the SAVIOUR of mankind;—
  Yet Jewry land with cruel hand,
  Both first and last His power envied;
*p* When He was born, they did Him scorn,
  And showed Him malice when He died.

*p* Princely Palace for our SAVIOUR
  In Judæa was not found,
  But blessed Mary's meek behaviour
  Patiently upon the ground
  Her BABE did place in vile disgrace,
  Where oxen in their stalls did feed;
  No midwife mild had this sweet CHILD,
  No woman's help at Mother's need.

*p* Kingly robes nor golden treasure
  Decked the Birthday of GOD's SON;
  No pompous train at all took pleasure
  To this KING of kings to run;
  No mantle brave could JESUS have
  Upon His cradle for to lie;
  Nor music's charms in nurse's arms
  To sing the BABE a lullaby.

*p* Yet as Mary sat in solace
  By our SAVIOUR's first beginning,
*cr* The Host of Angels from GOD's Palace
  Sounded sweet from Heaven singing;
  Yea, Heaven and earth for JESUS' Birth,
  With sweet melodious tunes abound,
*f* And everything for Jewry's KING,
  Upon the earth gave cheerful sound.

*mf* Now to Him that hath redeemed us
  By His Death on Holy Rood,
  And though poor sinners so esteemed us,
  That He bought us with His Blood,
*cr* Yield lasting fame, that still the Name
  Of JESUS may be honoured here;
*f* And let us say that Christmas Day
  Is still the best Day in the year.

---

*An excellent effect is produced by singing the last line of the last verse entirely in the major mode. It simply requires substituting ♮ for ♭ where an A or D occurs in all the parts.*

# Christmas Carols.

**Carol 6.**

hail His com - ing down to earth, Who rais - es us to Heaven.

  *f* A SAVIOUR! Sinners all around
    Sing, shout the wondrous word;
    Let every bosom hail the sound,
    A SAVIOUR! CHRIST the LORD!
     Noel, Noel, &c.

 *mf* For not to sit on David's throne
    With worldly pomp and joy,—
    He came for sinners to atone,
    And Satan to destroy;
   *f* Noel, Noel, &c.

    To preach the Word of Life Divine,
    To give the Living Bread,
    To heal the sick with Hand benign,
    And raise to life the dead.
     Noel, Noel, &c.

*mf* He preached, He (*pp*) suffered, bled and
*mf* Uplift 'twixt earth and skies;
    In sinners' stead was crucified,
    For sin a Sacrifice.
   *f* Noel, Noel, &c.

 *f* Well may we sing the SAVIOUR's Birth,
    Who need the Grace so given,
    And hail His coming down to earth,
    Who raises us to Heaven.
   *ff* Noel, Noel, &c.

# Christmas Carols.

### Carol 7.
**Verse.** *Moderato.*

*mf* Now lift the car-ol, men and maids, Now wake exultant singing; This day the WELL of LIFE first sprang, Who shall declare His springing? It is the Birth-day of our PEACE; This day for man the weary, The Everlasting SON of GOD Was born of blessed Mary.

No-el! No--el! Pro-claim the Saviour's Birth; He rais-es us to Heaven, O hail His com-ing down to earth.

*mf* He was not born in such sweet days,
　As we of yore remember;
　'Twas not the sunny summer time,
　　Oh! 'twas the cold December:
As shines the sun above the snows
　When nature's life is lying
Fast bound in winter's icy chain,
　So came He to the dying.
　　*f* Noel, Noel, &c.

*mf* He did not bring a royal train,
　A host no man might number,
Nor lay begirt by damask folds,
　Nor lulled by harp to slumber.
*p* Oh, He was wrapped in swathing bands
　Whose might o'erspans the heaven,
And that mean trough were oxen fed,
　For His first rest was given.
　　*f* Noel, Noel, &c.

*p* There were poor Shepherds in the field,
　Their flocks at midnight tending;
*cr* Then Heaven came down and brought for news,
　A rapture never ending;

*mf* So they went swift to Bethlehem,
　And saw—and told the story
Of Christ the Lord, a little Child,
　And Angels singing "Glory."
　　*f* Noel, Noel, &c.

*f* Not in the manger lies He now;
　Far o'er the sapphire portal
At God's right Hand of Power He sits
　Who was this day made mortal:
All in the highest, holiest place,
　Where there may dwell none other,
There our own Manhood sits enthroned,
　There is our Elder Brother.
　　*f* Noel, Noel, &c.

*f* The Birthday of our God and King—
　Lo! we are called to greet Him;
The Everlasting Bridegroom comes,
　Oh, go ye out to meet Him.
This is the end of all below,
　The crown of Love's best story;
Christ stands and knocks—oh, happy souls,
　Receive the King of Glory.
　　*ff* Noel, Noel, &c.

# Christmas Carols.

### Carol 8.

*mf* This Day a Child is born, Offspring of God's pure love, ... True Word, the Ever-lasting, And Wisdom from above! *f* No-el, No-el, No-el! All through the Day we sing. .. To greet the loving Sav-iour, Our Prophet, Priest, and King.

*mf* This Day is Jesus born,
    Made Flesh the Son of Man,
  Who erst did reign in glory,
    Before the world began!
    *f* Noel, &c.

*mf* This Day a Child is born,
    Creator, King, and Lord,—
*cr* In Majesty all glorious,
    By Heaven and earth adored
    *f* Noel, &c.

*mf* This Day the Light has come,
    Bright Beam of Peace and Love,—
  Way, Truth, and Life, sure Guidance,
    To our blest Home above!
    *f* Noel, &c.

*mf* This Day the Shepherd came
    To Shepherds in the field,
*dim* That we, His Sheep, might find Him,
    And He to death might yield.
    *f* Noel, &c.

*mf* One Day our Judge will come,
    And all shall hear His Voice,—
*cr* That Day, Sweet Jesus, bid us,
    With all Thy Sheep, rejoice!
    *f* Noel, &c.

# Christmas Carols.

### Carol 9.

*f* Let Heaven and earth re-joice and sing, Salute this happy Morn; The SAV-IOUR Which is CHRIST, our KING, And on this Day was born, The SAV-IOUR Which is CHRIST, our KING, And on this Day was born.

*f* Come let us join our hearts to GOD,
And thus exalt His Fame;
To save us all this BABE was born,
And JESUS is His Name.

*mf* Wise Men and Kings rich gifts did bring
To Bethlehem straightway;
Conducted by a leading Star,
Where CHRIST our SAVIOUR lay.

*ff* O LORD, to Thee all Glory be,
Whom Heaven and earth adore,
For our REDEEMER we will praise
This Day and Evermore.

# Christmas Carols.

Carol 10. (First Tune.)

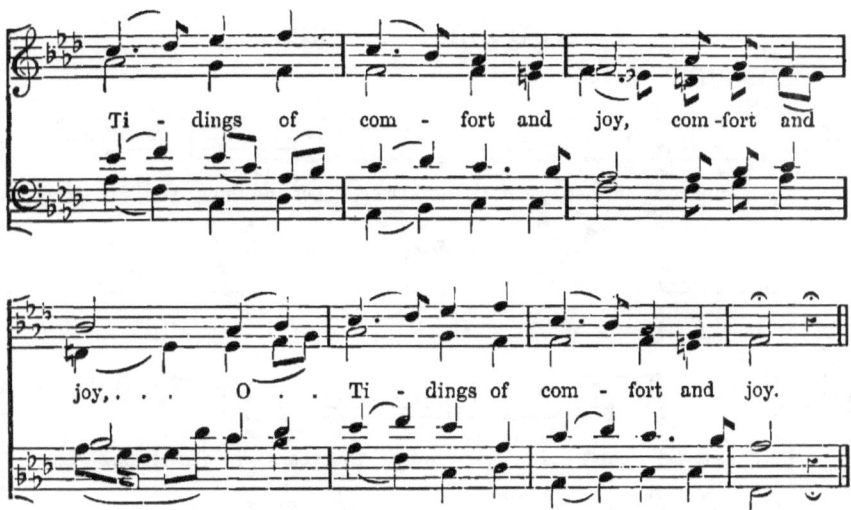

In Bethlehem, in Jewry,
  This Blessed BABE was born,
And laid within a Manger,
  Upon this happy Morn;
The which His Mother Mary
  Did nothing take in scorn.
    *f*  O Tidings, &c.

From GOD our Heavenly FATHER,
  A Holy Angel came,
And unto certain Shepherds
  Brought Tidings of the same,
How that in Bethlehem was born
  The SON of GOD by Name.
    *f*  O Tidings, &c.

"Fear not," then said the Angel,
  "Let nothing you affright,
This day is born the SAVIOUR
  Of a pure Virgin bright,
To free all those who trust in Him
  From Satan's power and might."
    *f*  O Tidings, &c.

*f*  The Shepherds at those Tidings
  Did much rejoice in mind,
And left their flocks a-feeding,
  In tempest, storm, and wind,
And went to Bethlehem straightway,
  This Blessed BABE to find.
    O Tidings, &c.

*mf* But when to Bethlehem they came,
  Where our dear SAVIOUR lay,
*dim* They found Him in a Manger,
  Where oxen feed on hay;
*p*  His Mother Mary kneeling,
  Unto the LORD did pray.
    *f*  O Tidings, &c.

*f*  Now to our GOD sing praises,
  All you within this place,
And with true love and brotherhood
  Adore our SAVIOUR's Grace;—
This Holy Tide of Christmas
  All others doth deface.
    *ff*  O Tidings, &c.

# Christmas Carols.

**Carol 10.** (Second Tune.)

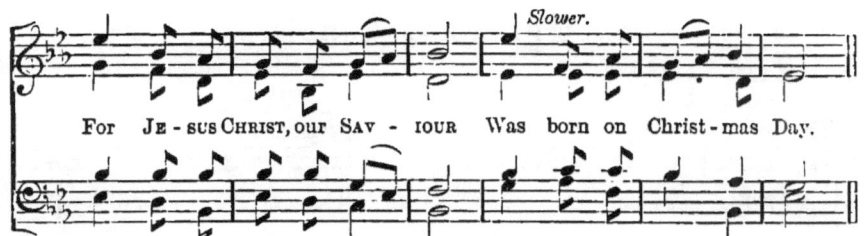

*mf* In Bethlehem, in Jewry,
    This Blessed BABE was born,
    And laid within a Manger,
    Upon this happy Morn;
    The which His Mother Mary
    Did nothing take in scorn.
       *f*  O Tidings, &c.

*mf* From GOD our Heavenly FATHER,
    A holy Angel came,
*cr* And unto certain Shepherds brought
    Glad Tidings of the same,
    How that in Bethlehem was born
    The SON of GOD by Name.
       *f*  O Tidings, &c.

*mf* "Fear not," then said the Angel,
    "Let nothing you affright.
    This Day is born the SAVIOUR
    Of a pure Virgin bright,
    To free all those who trust in Him
    From Satan's power and might."
       *f*  O Tidings, &c.

*f* The Shepherds at those Tidings
    Did much rejoice in mind,
    And left their flocks a-feeding,
    In tempest, storm, or wind,
    And went straightway to Bethlehem,
    This Blessed BABE to find.
       O Tidings, &c.

*mf* But when to Bethlehem they came,
    Where our dear SAVIOUR lay,
*dim* They found Him in a Manger,
    Where oxen feed on hay;
*p* His Mother Mary kneeling,
    Unto the LORD did pray.
       *f*  O Tidings, &c.

*f* Now to our GOD sing praises,
    All you within this place,
    And with true love and brotherhood
    Adore our SAVIOUR's Grace;—
    This holy Tide of Christmas
    All others doth deface.
       *ff*  O Tidings, &c.

# Christmas Carols.

## Carol 11.

sing, *p* And Peace up-on earth through the new-ly born KING.

*mf* From the Star of the Sea the glad SUNLIGHT hath shined,
Springs the LION of Judah from Naphtali's Hind,
The LIFE from the dying, the ROSE from the thorn,
The MAKER of all things of Maiden is born.
　　　*f* All glory, &c.

*mf* The manger of Bethlehem opens once more
*cr* The gates of that Eden where man dwelt of yore,
*p* And He Who is lying, a CHILD, in the Cave,
*f* Hath conquered the foeman, hath ransomed the slave.
　　　*f* All glory, &c.

*mf* In the midst of the Garden the TREE of LIFE stands,
And offers His twelve fruits to lips and to hands,
For the LORD of Salvation, the Gentiles' DESIRE,
Hath ta'en from the Cherubs their sword-blade of fire.
　　　*f* All glory, &c.

*mf* On the hole of the aspic the sucking CHILD plays,
And His Hand on the den of the cockatrice lays.
*cr* And the Dragon, which over a fallen world reigned,
By the SEED of the Woman is vanquished and chained.
　　　*f* All glory, &c.

*f* To Him Who hath loved us, and sent us His SON,
To Him Who the Victory for us hath won,
To Him Who sheds on us His Sevenfold rays,
Be Honour and Glory, Salvation and Praise.
　　　*ff* All glory, &c.

# Christmas Carols.

### Carol 12.

searched, and true they found it, Yet searched and true they found it.

*mf* The Son of God, the Eternal King,
That did us all salvation bring,
And freed the soul from danger;
He Whom the whole world could not take,
The Word, Which Heaven and earth did make,
*dim* Was now laid in a manger.

*mf* The Father's wisdom willed it so,
The Son's obedience knew no No,
Both wills were in one stature;
And as that wisdom had decreed,
*dim* The Word was now made Flesh indeed,
And took on Him our nature.

*mf* What comfort by Him do we win,
Who made Himself the price of sin,
To make us heirs of Glory!
To see this Babe, all innocence,
A Martyr born in our defence:—
*f* Can man forget the story?

# Christmas Carols.

**Carol 13.**

*mf* Christ-ians, car-ol sweet-ly, Up to-day and sing!

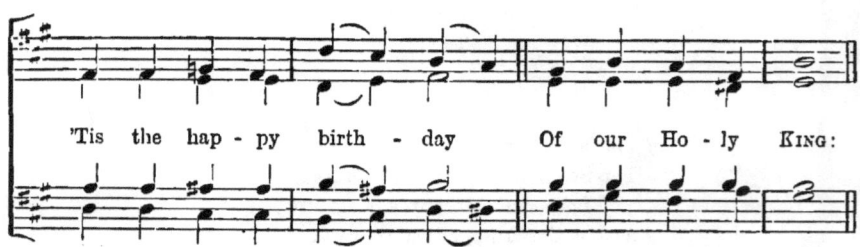

'Tis the hap-py birth-day Of our Ho-ly KING:

Haste we then to greet Him, *dim* Hum-bly fall-ing down,

*cr* While our hands en-twine Him, Dear-est BABE, a crown.

 *f* Crowds of snow-white Angels
  Throng the golden stair;
 All things are delightful,
  All things passing fair:
 Bells, clear music making,
  Peal the news to earth;
 Chimes within make answer,
  All is glee and mirth.

 *mf* Michael, at the manger,
  Bows his royal face;
 Gabriel, with lily,
  Hides transcendent Grace:
*f* For, dear friends, the Glory
  Of that lowly bed
 Overpowers the beauty
  On Archangels shed.

 *mf* Shall I tell of Joseph,
  Who, with rapt surprise,
 Sees the light from Godhead,
  Fill those infant eyes?
 Shall I sing of Mary,
  Who, upon her breast,
*dim* Cradles her CREATOR,
  Soothes Him to His rest?

 *mf* Angels, Mary, Joseph,
  Yes, I greet you all!
 Falling down in worship
  At the manger stall!
*cr* For you hail our MONARCH,
  Born a CHILD to-day;
*f* So, with you I worship,
  And my homage pay.

# Christmas Carols.

Carol 14.

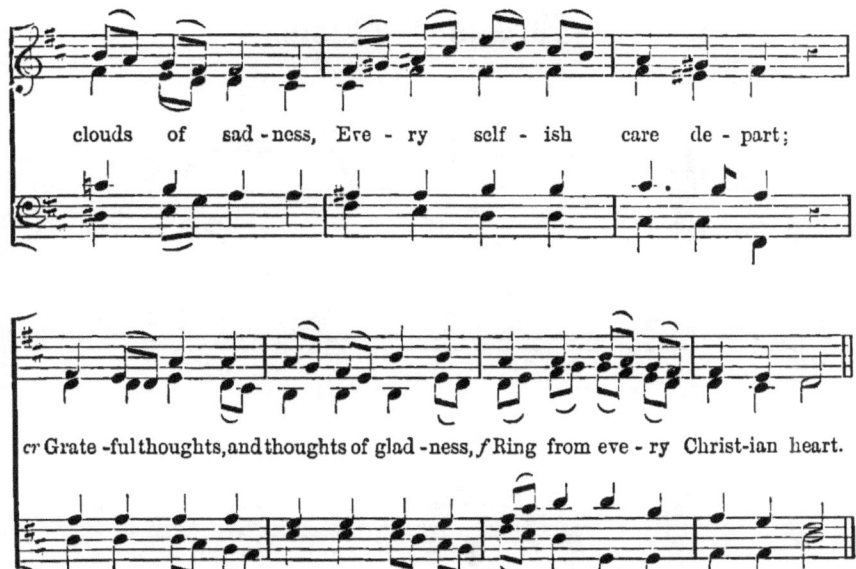

*f* Brightly in the holy chancel
　Leafy circles intertwine,
Telling how in Blessed JESUS
　Life and strength and joy combine.
As beneath the arch we enter
　Welcome words our coming bless,
For in Thee our hopes we centre,
　CHRIST, "THE LORD OUR RIGHTEOUSNESS."

*mf* In the nave each space is speaking
　Of the light which JESUS brought,
Of the freedom and the glory
　Which for all the world He wrought.
Wherefore, O ye congregation,
　Should your hearts be cold and dumb,
*cr* While the walls proclaim Salvation,
*ff* 　And, "Arise, thy LIGHT is come."

*mf* Listen to the old new message,
　At the Holy Table kneel;
Grudge not, when ye leave the Temple,
　To diffuse the warmth ye feel.
Life has time enough for sadness,
　Clouds too seldom pass away;
*cr* Only love and peace and gladness
*f* 　Should be named on Christmas Day.

# Christmas Carols.

**Carol 15.**

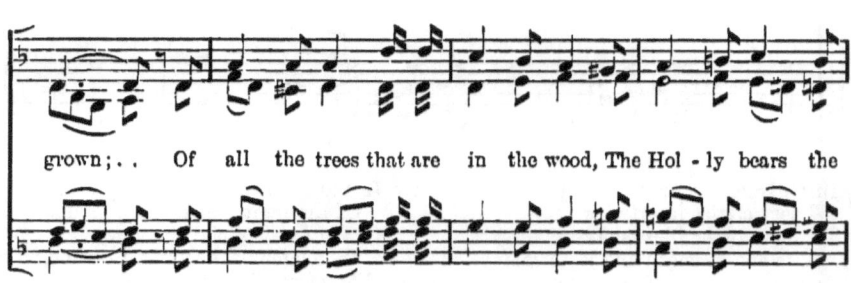

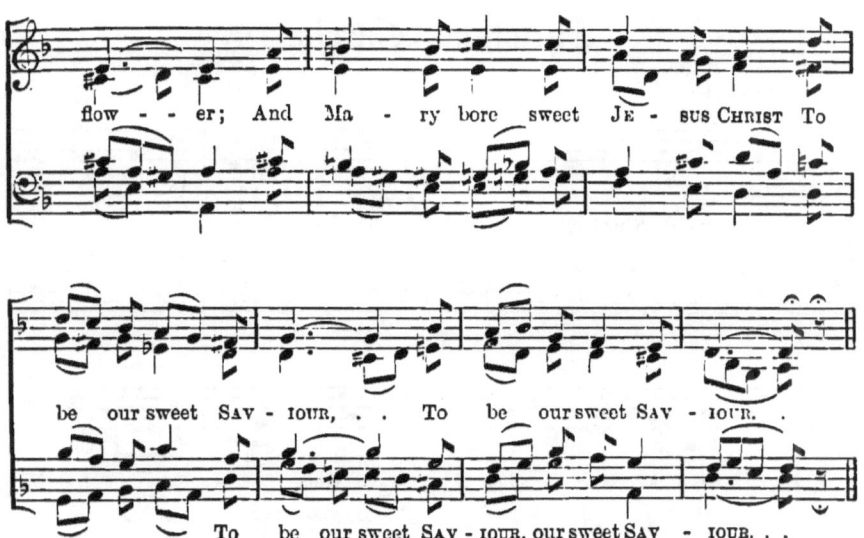

*mf* The Holly bears a berry
    As red as any blood ;
    And Mary bore sweet JESUS CHRIST
    To do poor sinners good.
    The Holly bears a prickle
    As sharp as any thorn ;
    And Mary bore sweet JESUS CHRIST
    On Christmas Day in the morn.

*mf* The Holly bears a bark
    As bitter as any gall ;
    And Mary bore sweet JESUS CHRIST
    For to redeem us all.
*cr* The Holly and the Ivy
    Now both are full well grown ;
    Of all the trees that are in the wood
*f*    The Holly bears the crown.

# Christmas Carols.

## Carol 16.
*Not too fast.*

> *f* Glory to God, as the Prophets foretold it,
>   Over the ages the Promise was cast;
> Paradise heard it, and now we behold it,
>   SEED of the Woman, we hail Thee at last.

> *f* Glory to God, for as dews of the morning,
>   Songs of Thy Birthday are filling the air;
> Shepherds of Bethlehem give us the warning,
>   CHILD of the Virgin, we welcome Thee there!

> *f* Glory to God, let the glad exultations
>   Sound through the world, bringing peace to the wise,
> Joy for all people—Desire of the nations!—
>   Echo the tidings in songs to the skies!

> *ff* We too, with Shepherd and Magi and Angel,
>   Prostrate before Thee our homage would bring;
> Hail Thee the SAVIOUR, the CHRIST, the EMMANUEL,
>   Own Thee our PROPHET, our PRIEST, and our KING.

# Christmas Carols.

### Carol 17.

*f* Hark! the Herald Angels sing Glory to the New-born KING

*p* Peace on earth and mercy mild, GOD and sinners reconciled.

*f* Joyful, all ye nations, rise, Join the triumph of the skies;

With th' Angelic Host proclaim CHRIST is born in Bethlehem.

*ff* Hark! the Herald Angels sing Glory to the New-born KING.

*mf* CHRIST, by highest Heaven adored,
CHRIST, the Everlasting LORD,
Late in time behold Him come,
*p* Offspring of a Virgin's womb.
Veiled in flesh the GODHEAD see;
Hail, the Incarnate DEITY!
Pleased as MAN with man to dwell,
JESUS, our EMMANUEL.
*f* Hark! the Herald Angels sing
Glory to the New-born KING.


*mf* Hail, the Heaven-born PRINCE of Peace,
Hail, the SUN of Righteousness!
Light and life to all He brings,
Risen with healing in His Wings.
*p* Now He lays His Glory by,
*cr* Born that man no more may die,
Born to raise the sons of earth,
Born to give them Second Birth.
*ff* Hark! the Herald Angels sing
Glory to the New-born KING.

# Christmas Carols.

### Carol 18.

Hark! hark! what News the Angels bring, Glad Tidings of the New-born King, the New-born King,— Born of a Maiden undefiled, Meet Mother of the Heavenly Child, the Heavenly Child.

*mf* Hail! Blessed Virgin, full of Grace,
Most favoured of our mortal race;
Whose sacred womb brought forth in one,
A Saviour, God, and Holy Son!

*mf* Man that was made from dust by God,
Had Paradise for his abode!
*p* But in a Manger at His Birth,
Lies God Who made the Heaven and [earth.

*p* Lo, in that Manger where He lies
Our faith discerns a Sacrifice;
And by His Birth may all men see
The pattern of humility.

*mf* Therefore, my God, my Saviour, King,
*cr* Thy praises I will ever sing,
In joyful Carols raise my voice,
*f* And in the Praise of God rejoice.

# Christmas Carols.

Carol 19.

*p* He Who built the starry skies
Low within a manger lies,
Stooping from His Throne sublime
High above the Cherubim.
  *ff* Hail, &c.

*mf* Say, ye wond'ring Shepherds, say,
What your joyful news to-day;
Wherefore have ye left your sheep?—
Wherefore fail your watch to keep?
  *ff* Hail, &c.

*p* "As we watched at dead of night
Lo! we saw a wondrous sight,—
Angels singing Peace on earth,
*cr* Telling of the SAVIOUR'S Birth."
  *ff* Hail, &c.

*mf* Haste we now to greet GOD'S CHILD,
Watch His Face so meek and mild;
Learn the Love of Heaven to see
In our LORD'S Humility.
  *ff* Hail, &c.

# Christmas Carols.

Carol 20.

|     |                                          |     |                                          |
| --- | ---------------------------------------- | --- | ---------------------------------------- |
| *mf* | " Fear not," said he, (for mighty dread  | *p* | " The Heavenly BABE you there shall find, |
|     | Had seized their troubled mind ; )       |     | To human view displayed,                 |
| *f*  | " Glad Tidings of great joy I bring      |     | All meanly wrapped in swathing bands     |
|     | To you and all mankind.                  |     | And in a Manger laid."                   |
|     |                                          |     |                                          |
| *mf* | " To you in David's town this day        | *p* | Thus spake the Seraph, and forthwith     |
|     | Is born, of David's line,                | *cr* | Appeared a shining Throng               |
|     | The SAVIOUR, Who is CHRIST the LORD,     |     | Of Angels, praising GOD, and thus        |
|     | And this shall be the sign :             | *f*  | Addressed their joyful song :           |

*ff*    " All Glory be to GOD on High,
*p*     And to the earth be Peace ;
*cr*    Goodwill, henceforth, from Heaven to men,
*f*      Begin and never cease."

# Christmas Carols.

Carol 21.

*mf* In Bethlehem City, in Jewry it was,
Where Joseph and Mary together did pass,
And there to be taxed, with many one mo',
For Cæsar commanded the same should be so. *f* Rejoice, &c.

*mf* But when they had entered the city so far,
The number of people so mighty was there,
That Joseph and Mary, whose substance was small,
*dim* Could get in the city no lodging at all.
*f* Rejoice, &c.

*p* Then they were constrained in a stable to lie,
Where oxen and asses they used to tie;
Their lodging so simple, they held it no scorn,
*cr* But 'gainst the next morning our SAVIOUR was born. *f* Rejoice, &c.

*p* The KING of all glory to this world was brought,
And small store of linen to wrap Him was wrought;—

When Mary had swaddled her young SON so sweet,
*pp* Within an ox manger she laid Him to sleep.
*f* Rejoice, &c.

*p* Then GOD sent an Angel from Heaven so high,
To certain poor Shepherds in fields where they lie,
*cr* And bid them no longer in sorrow to stay,
Because that our SAVIOUR was born on this day. *f* Rejoice, &c.

*mf* Then presently after, the Shepherds did spy
A number of Angels appear in the sky,
*cr* Who joyfully talked, and sweetly did sing,
*f* To GOD be all glory, our Heavenly KING.
Rejoice, &c.

*f* The Shepherds all glad did to Bethlehem go,
And when they came thither they found it was so:
And three Kings came from far, for they thought it most meet
To lay their rich offerings at JESUS CHRIST'S Feet. *ff* Rejoice, &c.

# Christmas Carols.

### Carol 22.

*mf* Good Christ-ians all ... with sweet ac - - cord, Sing praise to God ... on .. High, *cr* And with the Mo - ther of our Lord, *f* The Sav-iour mag-ni-fy, .. The Sav-iour mag-ni-fy.

*mf* He came for us upon this Morn,
    Thrice holy time of rest !
Jesus, the King of kings was born
    Of Ever Virgin blest.

*mf* Yet not with gems and gaudy show,
    With regal pomp arrayed,—
*dim* But in a Manger poor and low,
    The Lord of Life was laid.

*p* And from the Manger to the Cross
    The Holy, Undefiled,
*pp* Endured our sorrow, pain, and loss,
    Rejected and reviled.

*f* Then Carols to the welkin's ear
*cr*   Upraise, ye Christians all ;—
    The Angels tell us Christ is near,
*ff*   In this our Festival.

# Christmas Carols.

### Carol 23.

*Smoothly.*

*mf* I love to hear sweet voic-es sing, That Day of all the best, When ear-liest in the morn they bring The news of Christ-mas blest, *cr* And far a-way old e-choes ring, As bid-ding me to rest!

*mf* For then with waking thoughts intent
    My soul looks up on high,
And mingles musing with relent
    As fain 'twould see CHRIST nigh;
Hear for itself, ere time be spent,
*dim*    Peace from the azure sky!

*mf* But though no longer in our race
    By flesh the VIRGIN-BORN
Is known to us, yet JESUS' Grace
    Leaves not His Own forlorn;
*cr* Since now good Christians see His Face
*f*    By faith, on Christmas Morn!

*f* Then, come, ye faithful, great and small,
    Come hasten to the sight,
Where JESUS at our Festival
    Comes down, the shining LIGHT,
To fill all hearts, who hear His Call,
    With Glory beaming bright!

# Christmas Carols.

Carol 24.

*mf* For the Angel's Song at the Birth of Christ,
  With Tidings of joy began;
*cr* And it rang with a Glory to God in the Highest,
*dim* And a brotherhood true for man;
*mf* Yet 'twas winter time for the rich and poor,
  When the Shepherds came to Saint Mary's door.
  Yet 'twas winter, &c.

*mf* True Sages were they who to Bethlehem led, [Gold,—
  Brought Frankincense, Myrrh, and
  Which they offered to Christ on His Manger-bed,
*dim* With a reverent love untold.
  But 'twas winter time for the rich and poor, [door.
*mf* As the Wise Men knelt at Saint Mary's
  But 'twas winter, &c.

*mf* Cannot we make our offerings now to Christ's Need,
  When His Poor all around we see?
  "Inasmuch as to them we have done the deed,"
  He will say, "Ye have done it to Me."
*dim* 'Tis a wintry time for the rich and poor,
*f* Say who shall be driven from Christian door?
  'Tis a wintry, &c.

# Christmas Carols.

Carol 25.

 *mf* Very God of Very God,
   Light of Light Eternal;
 The Virgin's womb He hath not abhorred;
   True God Everlasting,
  *p* Not made but Begotten.
  *pp* O come let us adore Him!
  *p* O come let us adore Him!
*ff* O come let us adore Him, Christ, the Lord.


  *f* Sing, Chorus of Angels,
   Sing, in exultation,
*cr* Thro' Heaven's wide Court be your praises poured,
  *ff* To God in the Highest,
   Be honour and Glory;
  *pp* O come let us adore Him!
  *p* O come let us adore Him!
*ff* O come let us worship our God and Lord.


  *mf* Yea, Lord, we greet Thee,
   Born this happy Morning!
 For ever, O Christ, be Thy Name adored,
   True Word of the Father,
   Late in flesh appearing.
  *pp* O come let us adore Him!
  *p* O come let us adore Him!
*ff* O come let us worship our God and Lord.

# Christmas Carols.

Carol 26.

*mf* " Be not afraid when hearing the Choirs Seraphic sing ;
    This Night shall be the Birthtide of CHRIST the Heavenly KING :
*p*  He neither shall in housen be born, nor yet in hall ;
    Nor bed, nor downy pillow, but in an oxen stall.


    " He neither shall be clothed in purple nor in pall,
    But in the fair white linen that usen babies all.
    He neither shall be rocked in silver nor in gold ;
    But in a wooden Manger, that resteth on the mould."


*mf* As Joseph was a walking, thus did an Angel sing ;
    At night the Mother-maiden gave birth to CHRIST our KING.
    The Blessed Virgin wrapped Him from nightly winds, so wild ;
    The lowly Manger held Him Her wondrous Holy CHILD.


*mf* And marshalled on the mountain, the Angels raise their Song ;
*cr*  The Shepherds hear the story in anthems clear and strong.
    The Herald-hymn obeying, nor loth, nor yet afraid,
*dim*They seek the lowly dwelling, and there the CHILD is laid !


*mf* Then be ye glad, good people, this Night of all the year ;
*cr*  And light ye up your candles, His Star it shineth near.
    And all in earth and Heaven, our Christmas Carol sing :—
*ff*  Goodwill, and Peace, and Glory ! and all the bells shall ring.

# Christmas Carols.

**Carol 27.**

*mf* Let us now go to Beth-le-hem, To see the wondrous thing,— Ma-ry and Jo-seph and with them The BABE, our In-fant KING!— *cr* Bright Stars a-bove shine on, To light our speed-y way, *f* While An-gels sweet-ly car-ol in The Bless-ed Christ-mas Day.

*mf* Let us now go to Bethlehem,
    To see the wondrous thing,—
  Mary and Joseph and with them
    The BABE, our Infant KING!
  For we shall find on earth
    The Heaven of Heavens in Him,
  The Holy, Holy, Holy SON,
    Beneath\* the Cherubim.


*mf* Let us now go to Bethlehem,
    To see the wondrous thing,—
  Mary and Joseph and with them
    The BABE, our Infant KING;—
*cr*  His FATHER'S GLORY come
    To lift our hearts above.
  First loved by Him and Angel Hosts
*f*    We carol back His Love.


*mf* Let us then go to Bethlehem,—
    Faith's Star shall guide the way
  To JESUS cradled in His Church,
    This bright Appearing Day!
*cr*  There, LIGHT'S true LIGHT to Thee
    We sing with glad accord.
*ff*  For meet it is to celebrate
    Thy Birthday, JESUS LORD!


\* "Lower than the Angels awhile."—Heb. ii. **19.**

# Christmas Carols.

Carol 28.

town his Lord to see, The Babe in Glo-ry's morn - ing!

 *mf* Whom did ye see, ye Shepherds, say,
  On Christmas in the morning?
 Whose voice heard ye, this peaceful Day,
  Sweet singing in the morning?—
*cr* We heard their Carols in the sky,
  On Christmas in the morning;
 And saw the Angel Host on High
*f*  In robes of light, this morning!


 *mf* And Whom see ye, good Christians all,
  On Christmas in the morning?
 Whose voice hear we, this Festival,
  In tones of love and warning?—
*cr* We hear the Church, our Mother dear,
  On Christmas in the morning;
 And see Her Spouse for faith sees clear,
  The Incarnate Word, this morning.


 Then lift ye up your hearts aright,
  This Eucharistic morning!
 Come, come, where Altars beam with light,
  And choirs sing sweet, this morning:—
*ff* Glory to God, to God our King,
  On Christmas in the morning!
*p* Peace, Peace, let all good people sing,
*f*  Goodwill to men, this morning!

# Christmas Carols.

## Carol 29.

*mf* The Angel of the Lord came down in floods of dazzling light,
　　Above the brightness of the Sun when he goes forth with might;
　　His voice, it was so wondrous sweet, it made their hearts to thrill;
*f*　Now Glory be to God on High, and unto men Goodwill.

*mf* Fear not, he said, I bring glad news; in David's town this Morn,
　　To you and all the world a Saviour, Christ the Lord, is born,
　　This day is born the Saviour Christ, to save us from all ill;
*f*　Now glory be to God on High, and unto men Goodwill.

*mf* Then opened Heaven's Chancel, while the Shepherds gazed in fear,
*cr*　Out trooped the Choir of Angels; oh, the blessedness to hear!
*ff*　And loud they sang as though the Heavens were not enough to fill;
　　Now Glory be to God on High, and unto men Goodwill.

*f*　Oh, praise the Lord of Hosts Who sent His Singers sweet that night,
　　From the Holy place of Heaven, from the Choir that needs no light;
*mf* Let love this holy Season keep, let strife and turmoil cease,
*ff*　And Glory be to God on High, (*pp*) and on the earth be Peace.

# Christmas Carols.

**Carol 30.**

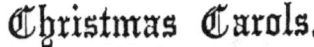

*f* Bright Angel Hosts . . are heard on High All sweetly singing o'er the plains; *cr* While mountains e- - cho in re- -ply *f* The bur- - -den of . . . . their joyous strains.

Say, Shepherds, why this Jubilee,
  What doth your rapturous mirth prolong?
Say, say, what may the Tidings be
  Which still inspire that Heavenly Song?

*mf* Come, come, to Bethlehem, come and see
  The CHILD Whose Birth the Angels sing;
*p* Come, come, adore on bended knee
  The INFANT CHRIST, The New-born KING!

  *p*  See there within a Manger laid
      JESUS, the LORD of Heaven and Earth!
  *cr* See, Saints and Angels lend their aid
  *f*   To celebrate the SAVIOUR's Birth!

Carol 31.

# Christmas Carols.

*f* Hark! the mu-sic of the Che-rubs, Bursting sud-den from the sky, Hark! the mu-sic of the Cherubs, Bursting sud-den from the sky; And a band of flam-ing Seraphs Tell-ing won-ders from on High, *cr* And a band of flam - ing Se - raphs *ff* Tell - - ing won - ders from on High.

*mf* See affrighted Shepherds gazing
On the bright celestial Host;
Whilst the dazzling light is blazing—
And they lie in wonder lost.
*mf* Cease your fears—a joyful story,—
Unto you is born a CHILD,—

*cr* Lo, He comes, the KING of Glory,
GOD to man is reconciled.
*p* Yes, He leaves His blissful Station,
And descends with man to dwell;
*cr* Praise Him in His Incarnation,
*f* He subdues the power of Hell.

*mf* Then to the watchful Shepherds it was told,
*cr* Who heard the Angelic Herald's voice, "Behold,
*f* I bring good Tidings of a Saviour's Birth
To you and all the nations of the earth;
This Day hath God fulfilled His promised Word,
This Day is born a Saviour, Christ the Lord,"

*f* He spake; and straightway the Celestial Choir
In hymns of joy, unknown before, conspire;
The praises of redeeming love they sang,
*ff* And Heaven's whole orb with Alleluias rang;
God's highest Glory was their Anthem still,
*p* Peace upon earth, and unto men Good-will.

*mf* To Bethlehem straight the enlightened Shepherds ran,
To see the wonders God had wrought for man;
*cr* Then to their flocks, still praising God, return,
And their glad hearts with holy rapture burn;
*f* To all the joyful Tidings they proclaim,
The first Apostles of the Saviour's Name.

*mf* Oh! may we keep and ponder in our mind
God's wondrous Love in saving lost mankind;
*p* Trace we the Babe, Who hath retrieved our loss,
From the poor Manger to the bitter Cross;
Tread in His steps, assisted by His Grace,
*mf* Till man's first Heavenly state again takes place.

*f* Then may we hope, the Angelic Hosts among,
To join, redeemed, a glad triumphant Throng:
He that was born upon this joyful Day
Around us all His Glory shall display:
*ff* Saved by His Love, incessant we shall sing
Eternal praise to Heaven's Almighty King.

# Christmas Carols.

## Carol 33.
*Smoothly*

*mf* What notes shall suit the Song Divine, That o'er the fields of Palestine, The wondering Shepherd hears? *p* When, 'mid the gloom of wintry night, When, 'mid the gloom of wintry night, *cr* A sudden burst of Heavenly light, A

sud-den burst of Heaven-ly light *f* O'er the still scene ap-pears!

*mf* A Glory thus transcending far
*dim* The full-orbed moon and brightest star
    First fills their hearts with fear;
*cr* But soon the Angel's soothing voice,
    In strains that bid the earth rejoice,
*f*    Salutes the raptured ear.

*f* "To you, this Day, a Saviour's born!
    Go, seek Him at the rising morn;
*mf*   For, found in humblest guise,
    In Bethlehem's walls, of David's race,
    A mean, but Heaven-protected place,
    The Glorious Infant lies."

*p* When now the voice of soothing sound
    Has ceased, and silence reigns around;
*cr*   Fresh on the listening ear,
    Breaks forth a new and rapturous song,
    And suddenly a shining Throng—
*f*    The Angelic Choirs appear!

*ff* Hark! how the starry arches ring!
    Glory to God on High, they sing;
*p*   And, to the sorrowing earth,
    Peace and Goodwill from Heaven they bear;
*cr* And in Seraphic strains declare
*f*    The Immortal Saviour's Birth.

# Christmas Carols.

Carol 34.

  *p* Still through the cloven skies they come,
   Love's banner all unfurled;
 *cr* And gladsome, too, their music floats
   O'er all the busy world:
  Above its sad and lowly plains
   Old echoes plaintive ring,
*mf* For ever o'er its Babel sounds
   The blessed Angels sing.


*mf* Yet with the woes of sin and strife
   The world has suffered long;
  Beneath the Angel-strain have rolled
   Two thousand years of wrong;
  And man at war with man hears not
   The love-song which they bring;
 *p* Oh! hush the noise, ye men of strife,
   And hear the Angels sing.


*pp* And ye, beneath life's crushing load,
   Whose forms are bending low,
  Who toil along the arduous way
   With painful steps and slow;
 *cr* Look now! for glad and joyous hours
   God's messengers will bring;
*mf* Oh! rest beside the weary road,
   And hear the Angels sing.

# Christmas Carols.

Carol 35.

of the skies!— A Sav - iour born To - day!

    *mf* Jesus, the God Whom Angels fear,
        Comes down to dwell with you;
*cr* To-day He makes His Entrance here,
*dim*  But not as Monarchs do!


*p*  Go, Shepherds, where the Infant lies,
      And see His humble Throne;—
*pp* With tears of joy in all your eyes,
      Go, Shepherds; "Kiss the Son!"


*f*  Glory to God, Who reigns above,
*p*    Let Peace surround the earth;
*f*  Mortals shall know their Maker's Love,
      At their Redeemer's Birth.

# Christmas Carols.

Carol 36.

*p*   "Thy body rest in slumber, child,
      Thy soul be free from sin!
    Thy Angel near and undefiled,
      Breathes all pure thoughts within.
*cr* The holy Christmas Tide is nigh,
      The Season of CHRIST's Birth;
*f* All Glory be to GOD on High,
*p*   And Peace to men on earth!


*mf* "For I and all the Heavenly Host
      Were keeping watch of old,
    And saw the Shepherds at their post,
      And all the sheep in fold.
*cr* Then told we with a joyful cry,
      The Tidings of CHRIST's Birth;
*f* All Glory be to GOD on High,
*p*   And Peace to men on earth!


*p*   "He bowed to all His FATHER's Will,
      The Lowly and the Meek;
    And year by year His Thoughts were still,
      Lost sinners for to seek.
    He did not come to strive nor cry,
*cr*   But ever from His Birth
*f* Gave Glory unto GOD on High,
*p*   And Peace to men on earth.


*mf* "Like Him be true, like Him be pure,
      Like Him be full of love;
    Seek not thine own, and so secure
      Thine own that is above,
*cr* And still when Christmas Tide draws nigh,
      Sing thou of JESUS' Birth;
*f* All Glory be to GOD on High,
*p*   And Peace to men on earth!"

# Christmas Carols.

## Carol 37.

*mf* High let us swell our tuneful notes, And join the Angelic Throng, .. For Angels no such love have known, To wake a cheerful song.

   *p*  Good-will to sinful men is shown,
        And Peace on earth is given,
        For lo! the Incarnate SAVIOUR comes,
        With messages from Heaven.

*mf* Justice and Grace, with sweet accord,
 *cr*  His rising Beams adorn;
  *f*  Let Heaven and earth in concert join,
        To us a CHILD is born.

 *ff*  Glory to GOD in highest strains,
        In highest worlds be given;
        His Will by us on earth be done,
        As it is done in Heaven.

**Carol 38.** Christmas Carols.

*mf* Hark! the full-voic'd Choir is singing, As the mid-night darkness flies;
Heavenly Angels now are bringing Peaceful Tidings from the skies.

CHORUS.
*f* Hail, O JESUS! Hail, O JESUS! SUN OF RIGHTEOUSNESS, arise! SUN OF RIGHTEOUSNESS, arise!

*mf* Yes, behold the Day of Glory,
   Dawn at length for all the earth;
List, the Cherubs tell the story,—
   "This the Day of JESUS' Birth."
  *f* Hail, O JESUS!
DAY-SPRING from on High, shine forth!

*p* Lo, He comes! His Throne the Manger,
   Shepherds, seek His Shrine the Stall;
Ox and ass behold the STRANGER,*

GOD, Who made and governs all!
  *f* Hail, O JESUS!
Hail Thy glorious festival!

*ff* Mortals, raise your loudest voices,
   JESUS lifts on high your horn;
Earth redeemed To-day rejoices,
   For To-day her LORD is born!
  Hail, O JESUS!
Hail, all hail this Sacred Morn!

*"I was a STRANGER, and ye took Me not in."—S. Matt. xxv. 43.*

# Christmas Carols.

Carol 39.

*mf* Once again the Holy Night
    Breathes its blessing tender;
    Once again the Manger Light
    Sheds its gentle splendour;
*cr* O could tongues by Angels taught
    Speak our exultation
    In the Virgin's CHILD that brought
    All mankind Salvation!

*mf* Welcome Thou to souls athirst,
    Fount of endless pleasure;
    Gates of hell may do their worst,
    While we clasp our Treasure;
*cr* Welcome, though an age like this
    Puts Thy Name on trial,
    And the Truth that makes our bliss
    Pleads against denial!

*mf* Yea, if others stand apart,
    We will press the nearer;
    Yea, O best fraternal Heart,
    We will hold Thee dearer;
*cr* Faithful lips shall answer thus
    To all faithless scorning,
*ff* "JESUS CHRIST is GOD with us,
    Born on Christmas morning."

*f* So we yield Thee all we can,
    Worship, thanks, and blessing;
*p* Thee true GOD, and Thee true Man,
    On our knees confessing;
*cr* While Thy Birthday Morn we greet
    With our best devotion,
    Bathe us, O most true and sweet!
    In Thy Mercy's ocean.

*pp* Thou that once, 'mid stable cold,
    Wast in babe-clothes lying,
    Thou whose Altar-veils enfold
    Power and Life undying,
    Thou whose Love bestows a worth
    On each poor endeavour,
*f* Have Thou joy of this Thy Birth
*ff*    In our praise for ever.

# Christmas Carols.

Carol 40.

f  The answering hills of Palestine
     Send back the glad reply,
    And greet from all their holy heights
     The DAY-SPRING from on High;
mf O'er the blue depths of Galilee
     There comes a holier calm,
    And Sharon waves in stately praise
     Her silent groves of palm.
       ff  Glory to GOD on High!

f  Glory to GOD!—the lofty strain
     The realm of ether fills:
    How sweeps the song of solemn joy
     O'er Judah's ancient hills!
cr Glory to GOD!—the sounding skies
ff    Loud with the anthems ring;
p  Peace to the earth, good-will to men,
     From Heaven's Eternal KING!
       ff  Glory to GOD on High!

mf Light on thy hills, Jerusalem!
     The SAVIOUR now is born;
    More bright on Bethlehem's joyous plains
     Breaks the first Christmas Morn,
cr And brighter on Moriah's brow
     Crowned with her temple towers;
    Proclaiming from that sacred height
     Salem's true LIGHT and ours.
       ff  Glory to GOD on High!

f  This Day shall Christian tongues be mute?
     Shall Christian hearts be cold?
    Oh, catch the anthem that from Heaven
     O'er Judah's mountains rolled,
    When nightly burst from Seraph harps
     The high and welcome lay—
    "Glory to GOD! (<i>p</i>) on earth be Peace!
ff    Salvation comes to-day!"
       ff  Glory to GOD on High!

# Christmas Carols.

**Carol 41.**
VERSE.  *Cantoris only.*

*Decani verse.*    *f*   "Glory in the Highest, Glory,"
                 Thus they chant their joyful strain;
                "Glory in the Highest, Glory,
           *p*   Peace on earth, Good-will to men."
                                Hark, &c.

*Cantoris verse.*    *mf* With their blessed Alleluias,
                 Hear what wondrous things they tell,
           *f*   How lost man has now a SAVIOUR,
                 Born to conquer death and hell.
                                  Hark, &c.

*Decani verse.*    *mf* Born Thy people to deliver,
                 JESU! from the death of sin;
                 Born to make us Thine for ever,—
                 Still abide our souls within!
                                Hark, &c.

*Cantoris verse.*    *f*   SON of GOD! Most Holy JESU!
                 Endless Glory be to Thee;
                 To the FATHER and the SPIRIT,
                 Now and through Eternity.
                                Hark, &c.

# Christmas Carols.

Carol **42.**

    *mf* This favour Christ vouchsafed for our sake;
  *dim* To buy us Thrones, He in a Manger lay;
       Our weakness took, that we His Strength might take,
   *pp*   And was disrobed, that He might us array;
       Our flesh He wore, our sins to wear away;
       Our curse He bore, that we escape it may;
       And wept for us that we might sing for aye.
    *cr* With Angels, therefore, sing again;
    *ff* To God on High all Glory be,
    *p* For Peace on earth bestoweth He,
       And sheweth favour unto men.

# Christmas Carols.

**Carol 43.**

*mf* Never fell melodies half so sweet
  As those which are filling the skies;
*f* And never a Palace shone half so fair,
  As the Manger-bed where our SAVIOUR lies
No night *in the* year *is* half so dear
  As this, which has *ended* our sighs.

*mf* Now *a* new Power has come *on the* earth,
  A match for the armies of hell:
*f* A CHILD is born Who shall con*quer the* foe,
  *And* all the spirits of *wicked*ness quell:
For Mary's SON is the Mighty ONE
  *Whom the* Prophets of GOD foretell.

*mf* The stars of heaven still shine *as at* first
  They gleamed on this wonderful night;
*f* The bells of the City of GOD peal out,
  And the Angels' song *still* rings *in the* height;
And love still turns where the GODHEAD burns,
*dim* *Veiled in* Flesh *from* fleshly sight.

*mf* Faith *sees no* longer the stable f r,
  The pavement of sapphire is there;
*f* The clear light of Heaven streams out *to the* world;
  *And Angels of* GOD *are* crowding *the air;*
*dim* And Heav'n and earth, through the Spotless Birth,
  *Are at* peace on this night so fair.

Verses 2, 3, and 5 begin on the second chord, *i.e.* at the beginning of the bar. Monosyllables in italics should be sung to two notes, and di-syllables to one note or two notes slurred. See Treble part, Edition E or F.

# Christmas Carols.

Carol 44.

*mf* 'Twas Blessed Mary, daughter pure
Of Saintly mother Anne,
That brought into this sinful world
The SAVIOUR GOD made Man.

*p* She laid Him lowly in the stall
At ancient Bethlehem;
And ox and ass did also share
The humble roof with them.

*mf* And Joseph, Mary's holy Spouse
Was near to tend the CHILD,—
And duteously protect from harm
The Virgin Mother mild.

*mf* The Angels hovered round the place,
And sang the Heavenly Song—
O come ye, come ye, and adore
The SAVIOUR promised long.

*p* And now, behold, that Manger poor
*cr* Henceforth becomes a Throne;
For He Whom Blessed Mary bore
*f* Was JESUS GOD's Own SON!

*f* O come, then, Christians, let us join
The bright and Heavenly Host,
*cr* And sing the praise of FATHER, SON,
And of the HOLY GHOST.

# Christmas Carols.

Carol 45.

*f* No-el, No-el, No-el, No-el! *mf* This is the sa-lu-ta-tion of the An-gel Ga-bri-el. *cr* Ti-dings true I bring to you Sent from the T<small>RI</small>-<small>NI</small>-<small>TY</small>,... By Ga-bri-el to Na-za-reth, Ci-ty of Ga-li-lee, *mf* A

*f* Noel, Noel, Noel, Noel!
*mf* This is the Salutation of the Angel Gabriel.
*cr* Tidings true I bring to you, ye Shepherds round about,
    In Bethlehem the LORD is born, Go, Shepherds Seek Him out!
*p* Ye there shall find the Holy CHILD, laid in a Manger poor!
*f* Go, tell abroad these Tidings; Go, worship and adore.


*f* Noel, Noel, Noel, Noel!
*mf* This is the Salutation of the Angel Gabriel.
*cr* Tidings true I bring to you, with me the Angels sing,
    In David's City is the LORD, the SAVIOUR, CHRIST, the KING!
*ff* Then men and Angels, carol on your loudest praise again,
    To GOD on High all Glory, (*pp*) and Peace below to men!

# Christmas Carols.

Carol 46.

*mf* Go ye to the forest,
    Where the myrtles grow,
  Where the pine and laurel
    Bend beneath the snow :
  Gather them for JESUS ;
    Wreathe them for His Shrine ;
*cr* Make His Temple glorious
    With the box and pine.
        *ff* Carol, carol.

*mf* Carol, carol, Christians,
    Like the Magi now,
  Ye must lade your caskets
    With a grateful vow :
  Ye must have sweet incense,
    Myrrh, and finest gold,
*p* At our Christmas Altar,
    Humbly to unfold.
        *ff* Carol, carol.

*mf* Wreathe your Christmas garland,
    Where to CHRIST we pray ;
  It shall smell like Carmel
    On our festal day ;
  Libanus and Sharon
    Shall not greener be,
*cr* Than our holy chancel
    On CHRIST's Nativity.
        *ff* Carol, carol.

*f* Blow, blow up the trumpet,
    For our solemn Feast ;
  Gird thine armour, Christian,
    Wear thy vesture, priest !
  Go ye to the Altar,
    Pray, with fervour pray,
  For JESUS' Second Coming,
    And the Latter Day.
        *ff* Carol, carol.

*mf* Give us Grace, oh SAVIOUR,
    To put off in might
  Deeds and dreams of darkness,
    For the robes of light !
  And to live as lowly
    As Thyself with men ;
*cr* So to rise in glory
    When Thou com'st again !
        *ff* Carol, carol.

  *mf* Carol, sweetly carol,
    As when the Angel throng,
    O'er the vales of Judah,
 *cr*  Awoke the Heavenly song:
 *f* Carol, sweetly carol,
 *p*  Goodwill, and Peace, and Love,
 *ff* Glory in the Highest
    To God Who reigns above.
     *f* Carol, &c


 *f* Carol, sweetly carol,
    The happy Christmas time :
    Hark! the bells are pealing
    Their merry, merry chime :
 *cr* Carol, sweetly carol,
    Ye shining ones above,
    Sing in loudest numbers,
    Oh, sing redeeming Love.
     *ff* Carol, &c.

# Christmas Carols.

Carol 48.

laud, The BABE, the BABE, the SON of Ma - ry!

*p* Why lies He in such mean estate,
    Where ox and ass are feeding?
*dim* Good Christian, fear; for sinners here
    The silent WORD is pleading:
*pp* Nail, Spear, shall pierce HIM through,
    The Cross be borne, for me, for you;
*mf* Hail, hail, the WORD made Flesh,
    The BABE, the SON of Mary!


*mf* So bring Him incense, gold, and myrrh,
    Come peasant, King, to own Him:
    The KING of kings Salvation brings,
*cr*   Let loving hearts enthrone Him.
    Raise, raise the song on high,
    The Virgin sings her lullaby:
*f* Joy, joy, for CHRIST is born,
    The BABE, the SON of Mary!

| f | Glory to God, in Highest Heaven, |
| p | To men of good-will Peace,— |
| mf | The Angel said,—A Son is given, |
| cr | Whose kingdom shall increase. |

Then Carols sing, good Christians all,
With Angel Hosts above,—
For Christ we keep the festival,
And Jesus owns our love.

f And thus let all the ransomed earth
 Resound with harmony;
 For our Redeemer's humble Birth
ff Laud we the One in Three.

# Christmas Carols.

**Carol 50.**

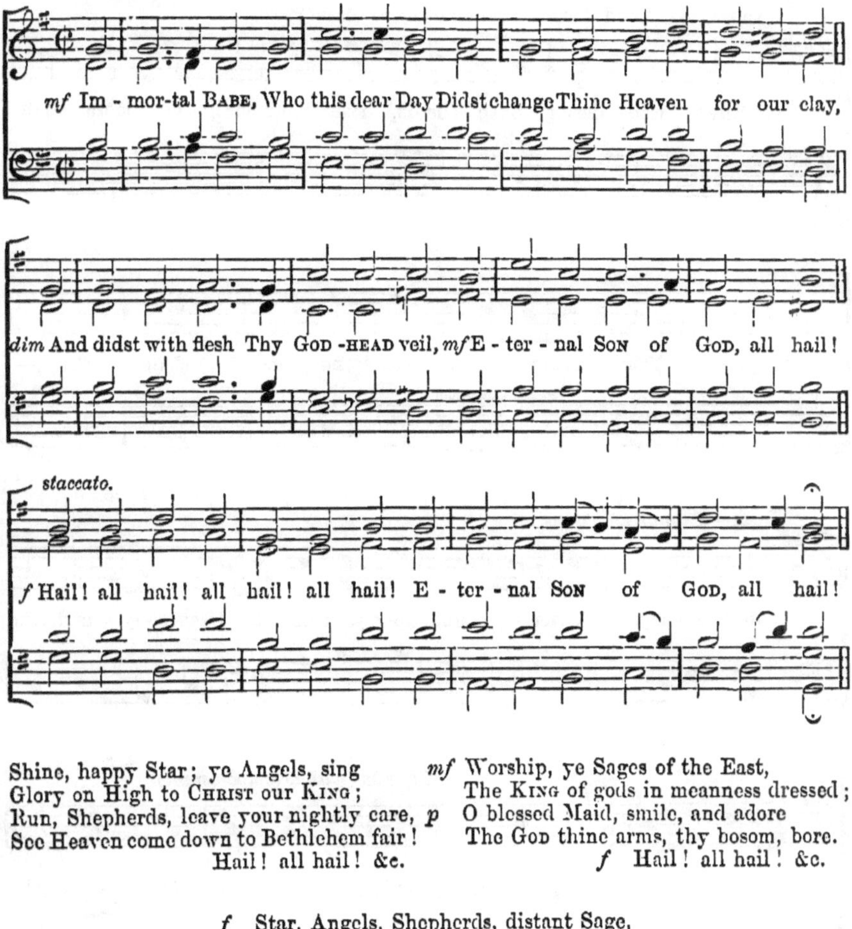

*mf* Im-mor-tal BABE, Who this dear Day Didst change Thine Heaven for our clay,

*dim* And didst with flesh Thy GOD-HEAD veil, *mf* E-ter-nal SON of GOD, all hail!

*staccato.*

*f* Hail! all hail! all hail! all hail! E-ter-nal SON of GOD, all hail!

    Shine, happy Star; ye Angels, sing  
    Glory on High to CHRIST our KING;  
    Run, Shepherds, leave your nightly care, *p*  
    See Heaven come down to Bethlehem fair!  
        Hail! all hail! &c.

*mf* Worship, ye Sages of the East,  
    The KING of gods in meanness dressed;  
*p* O blessed Maid, smile, and adore  
    The GOD thine arms, thy bosom, bore.  
    *f* Hail! all hail! &c.

*f* Star, Angels, Shepherds, distant Sage,  
    Thou Virgin, blest of every age,  
    Restored frame of Heaven and earth,  
    Joy in your dear REDEEMER's Birth.  
        Hail! all hail! &c.

# Christmas Carols.

## Carol 51.

**DUET—ALTO and TENOR** (*without accompaniment*).

*mf* Rise, won-dering Shep-herds, rise, Your sheep no more shall stray,— *cr* Your sheep . . . . . no more shall stray;—

**DUET—TREBLE and BASS.**

*mf* Tune your harps to Heaven-ly sound, Tune your harps to Heaven-ly sound, And hail this hap-py Day. *f* This is JE-SUS' Na-tal Day!

**CHORUS** (*with accompaniment*).

*f* Joy, joy, to all the world!
    This Day no grief appears,
    CHRIST, our Blessed LORD, is come,
    To dry up all our tears.
        This, &c.


*f* Glory to GOD above,
    Praise Him with heart and voice;
    Now the Gentiles' Light is come,
    Let all mankind rejoice!
        *ff*    This, &c.

# Christmas Carols.

**Carol 52.**

RECIT. TREBLE. *Rather slow.*

*mf* There were Shepherds, a-bid-ing in the field, a-bid-ing in the field, keeping watch, keeping watch o-ver their flocks by night. And the An-gel said un-to them, Fear not, Fear not; for, be-

# Christmas Carols.

## Carol 53.
DUET. *Trebles and Altos.*

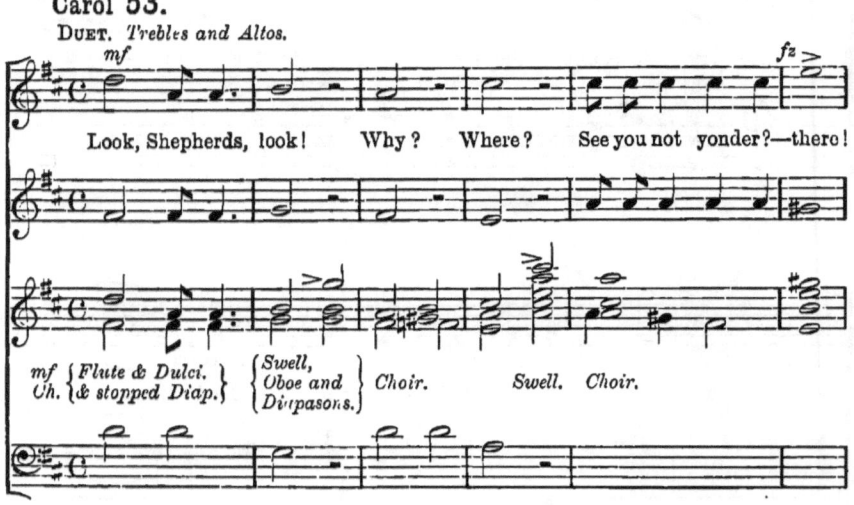

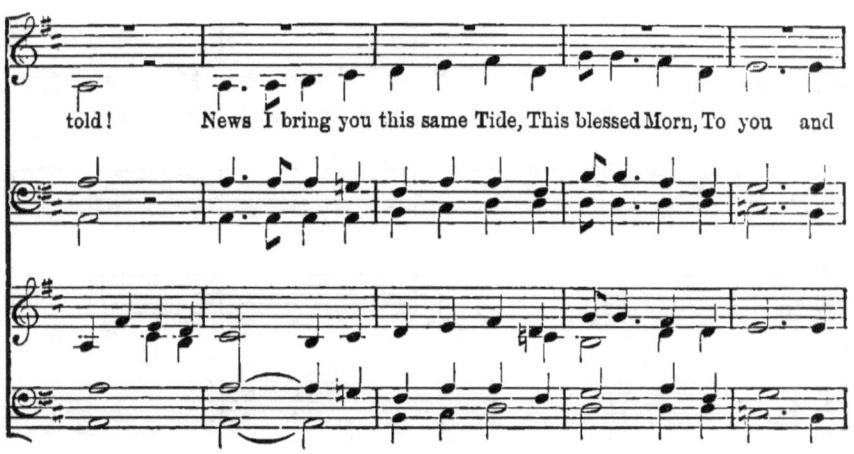

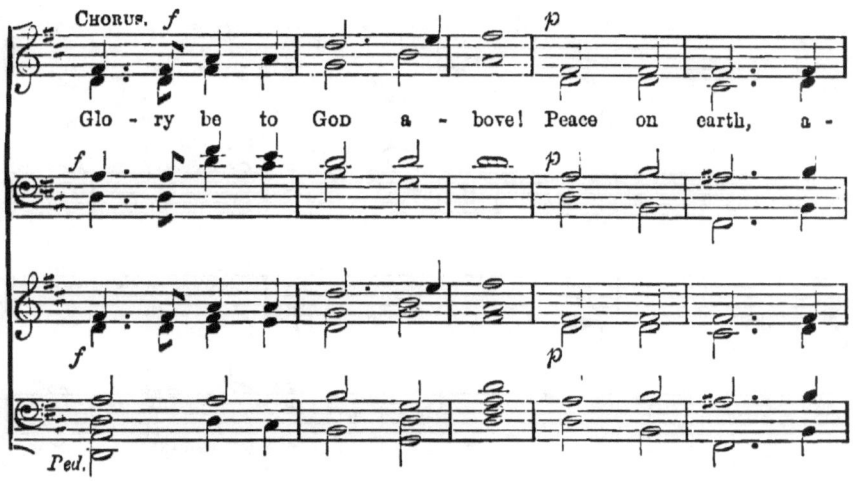

# Christmas Carols.

Carol 54. (First Tune.)

108

*mf* Is this, ye holy Shepherds,
    The mighty new-born KING?
This CHILD, so sweet and gentle,
    Can He such rapture bring?
*cr* O yes! He comes, the SAVIOUR
    Of sinful earth forlorn;
*f* Then shout with joy, ye mortals,
*ff*    For JESUS CHRIST is born!


*mf* The cruel, cruel foeman
    This CHILD shall overthrow;
Full soon, the fierce destroyer,
    His LORD's stern might shall know:
Of all His boasted power
    Soon to be roughly shorn;
*f* Then shout with joy, ye mortals,
*ff*    For JESUS CHRIST is born!


*p* But say, sweet Virgin-mother,
    The CHILD upon Thy breast,
Will He receive young children,
    And share with them His rest?
*mf* O yes! He will with glory
    Both old and young adorn;
*f* Then shout with joy, ye mortals,
*ff*    For JESUS CHRIST is born!


*f* Rejoice then, youths and maidens,
    Old men and children, too;
*cr* Lift up your cheerful voices,
    With bliss and rapture true!
*ff* Ring out, ye towers and steeples!
    Blow trumpet, pipe, and horn!
And shout with joy, ye mortals,
*fff*    For JESUS CHRIST is born!

# Christmas Carols.

Carol 54. (Second Tune.)

*mf* A shout of mighty triumph Through nature's realm is heard,
A shout which calls cre-a-tion To hail th' In-car-nate Word.
*f* A-way with clouds and dark-ness! All hail, thrice bless-ed Morn;
Sing out with joy, ye mor-tals, *ff* For Je-sus Christ is born!

*mf* Is this, ye holy Shepherds,
    The mighty new-born KING?
This CHILD, so sweet and gentle,
    Can He such rapture bring?
*cr* O yes! He comes, the SAVIOUR
    Of sinful earth forlorn;
*f* Then shout with joy, ye mortals,
*ff*    For JESUS CHRIST is born!

*mf* The cruel, cruel foeman
    This CHILD shall overthrow;
Full soon, the fierce destroyer,
    His LORD's stern might shall know:
Of all His boasted power
    Soon to be roughly shorn;
*f* Then shout with joy, ye mortals,
*ff*    For JESUS CHRIST is born!

*p* But say, sweet Virgin-mother,
    The CHILD upon Thy breast,
Will He receive young children,
    And share with them His rest?
*mf* O yes! He will with glory
    Both old and young adorn;
*f* Then shout with joy, ye mortals,
*ff*    For JESUS CHRIST is born!

*f* Rejoice then, youths and maidens,
    Old men and children, too;
*cr* Lift up your cheerful voices,
    With bliss and rapture true!
*ff* Ring out, ye towers and steeples!
    Blow trumpet, pipe, and horn!
And shout with joy, ye mortals,
*fff*    For JESUS CHRIST is born!

# Christmas Carols.

Carol 55.

snow; From the still and tranquil heaven,'Midst the howl-ing winds that blow.

  *mf* Lo! the King of Angels bendeth,
  *dim* Comes and steps below their choirs,
   Down the ten degrees the shadow
   On the dial-plate retires.*
  *p* Lo! for man condemned to perish
   Jonathan puts off his crown;
  Lo! he strips himself to furnish
   David with his princely gown,
  With his robes the doomed one 'scapeth
   Safely from the Father's frown.†

  *p* Lo! the Highest is made lowest,
   Lo! the Almighty is made weak:
  Lo! the Light of lights, in darkness,
   Shepherds in a stable seek.
  Lo! the King becomes the subject:
   Lo! the One Eternal—born!
  Lo! Creation's Source—a creature!
   And the Honoured suffers scorn.
  Lo! the Sun, to earth declining,
   Of his golden rays is shorn.

*p*  Wherefore is the High debased?
*f*   But that we may lifted be;
*p*  Wherefore comes the Sun among us?
*f*   But that blinded eyes may see.
*p*  Wherefore is the King made subject?
*f*   But that we through Him may reign;
*p*  Wherefore shines the Light in darkness?
*f*   But to illumine man again,
  Who so long had crouched imprisoned,
   Bound by Satan's cruel chain.

* 2 Kings xx. 11. The descent of the shadow on the dial of Ahaz down ten degrees, is a type of the descent of Christ below the nine degrees of angels, "Being made a little lower than the angels."
† 1 Sam. xviii. 4. Jonathan another type of Christ.

# Christmas Carols.

**Carol 56.**

*Choir only, unaccompanied.*

*mf* 1. The WORD made Flesh, right re-ve-rent-ly, The ris-ing of our Sun, we sing, Of Ma-ry born with us to be Em-man-u-el our GOD and KING.

*Full Choir and Congregation, with Organ Accompaniment.*

2. *f* Good news! the Book of Life's unsealed,
   *p* To men on earth His peace He brings,
   *cr* Through ages promised, now revealed,
       He comes with healing on His wings.

3. *f* Then Beth-le-hem of Is-ra-el, The

* The *odd* verses are to be sung by the Cantors, Quartett, Semi-Choir, or *unaccompanied* full choir: the *even* verses by the full choir and congregation, with organ accompaniment.

no - blest ci - ty, praise to thee; Known where - so - e'er the Church shall tell Of Jesus Christ's Na - ti - vi - ty.

4. *p* No courtly hall received the Maid, Our KING was in a manger laid;
The Mother of the Holy CHILD, *cr* A wondrous star above Him smiled.

*mf* 5. Who with His hands heaven's cur - tain spread, *p* In swad - dling clothes doth meek - ly rest; *mf* Who life on all cre - a - tion shed, *p* Hangs fee - bly on a mo - ther's breast.

6. *p* Be present, angel hosts, adore *cr* Who comes creation to restore,
The world's CREATOR and your KING. *f* And conquered man to victory bring.

10. *mf* The new-born God exhorts you flee
The world that wanes and waxes old;
An exile here in poverty
He bids you scorn its proffered gold.

12. *p* When ye with wondering faith adore
The Gentiles' King, on Mother's knee;
When hearts with love are flowing o'er,
Prostrate before His Majesty,

* This ♮ may be sung ♭, as in the original.

13. *p* Then Mary lifts her Holy Child, With rais-ed hand He makes the sign, *dim* Par-doned we bend, and re - con - ciled, *pp* His peace is ours, peace all Di - vine.

14. *mf* CREATOR, Thou Who sought'st this place
Of woe, in human form, we pray
Make us to see Thee, face to face,
Enthroned in Thine eternal day.

A — — — — — — — — — — — — men.

## Carol 57. Christmas Carols.

*mf* Sing ye the songs of praise; Christ-mas is come! High your glad voic-es raise; Christ-mas is come! Cast world-ly cares a-way, Wor-ship, and hom-age pay, *cr* Welcome the bless-ed day, *f* Christ-mas is come!

*mf* This day in Bethlehem
　　　　JESUS was born!
KING of Jerusalem,
　　　　JESUS was born!
SUN of all righteousness,
Shining with blessedness,
Healing our wretchedness,
　　*f* JESUS was born!

*mf* Perfect GOD, perfect man,
　　　　Born in the world!
Working His gracious plan,
　　　　Born in the world!
*dim* A manger must be His cot,
Other room He had not;
Such was His lowly lot,
　　*mf* Born in the world!

*mf* Be humble, sons of men;
　　　　Humble was CHRIST!
Pride ill becomes you when
　　　　Humble was CHRIST!
Never forsake Him,
Your righteousness make Him,
As best model take Him;
　　　　Humble was CHRIST!

*mf* Cleanse us from all our sin,
　　　　SAVIOUR Divine!
Make our thoughts pure within,
　　　　SAVIOUR Divine!
*cr* Lo! now the herald sound
Carols the love profound,
Telling of JESUS found,
　　*f* SAVIOUR Divine!

*mf* Save through Thy merit,
　　　　Great PRINCE of Peace!
Give Thy good SPIRIT,
　　　　Great PRINCE of Peace!
Let not Thy love depart,
But holy gifts impart,
Born into every heart,
　　*p* Great PRINCE of Peace!

# Christmas Carols.

Carol 58.

*p* He came down to earth from Heaven,
  Who is God and Lord of all,
  And His shelter was a stable,
  And His cradle was a stall;
    With the poor, and mean, and lowly,
    Lived on earth our Saviour holy.


*mf* And through all His wondrous Childhood,
  He would honour and obey,
  Love and watch the lowly Maiden,
  In whose gentle arms He lay;
    Christian children all must be
    Mild, obedient, good, as He.


*mf* For He is our childhood's pattern,
  Day by day like us He grew,
  He was little, weak, and helpless,
*dim* Tears and smiles like us He knew,
  And He feeleth for our sadness,
*f*  And He shareth in our gladness.


*mf* And our eyes at last shall see Him,
  Through His own redeeming love,
*cr* For that Child, so dear and gentle,
  Is our Lord in Heaven above;
    And He leads His children on
    To the place where He is gone


*p* Not in that poor lowly stable,
  With the oxen standing by,
  We shall see Him; (*cr*) but in Heaven,
  Set at God's right Hand on High;
    When like stars His children crowned,
*f*  All in white, shall wait around.

# Christmas Carols.

Carol 59.

*mf* 'Twas in the days when far and wide
  Men owned the Cæsar's sway,
 That his decree went forth, that all
  A certain tax should pay.
 Then from their home in Nazareth's vale,
  Obedient to the same,
 With Mary, his espoused wife,
  The saintly Joseph came.

*p* A stable and a manger, where
  The oxen lowed around,
 Was all the shelter Bethlehem gave,
  The welcome that they found!
*mf* Yet blessed among women was
  That holy mother-maid,
*dim* Who on that night her First-born Son
  There in the manger laid.

*p* The King of kings, and Lord of lords,
  E'en from His very Birth,
 Had not a place to lay His Head,
  An outcast in the earth:
*dim* And yet we know that little Babe
  Was tender to the touch,
 And weak as other infants are;
*pp* He felt the cold as much!

*p* In swaddling bands she wrapped Him round,
  And smoothed His couch of straw,
 While unseen Angels watched beside,
  In mute, adoring awe.
*cr* How softly did they fold their wings
  Beneath that star-lit shed,
 While eastern Sages from afar
*f*  The new-born radiance led!

*mf* And thus it is, from age to age,
  That as this night comes round,
 So sweetly, underneath the moon,
  The Christmas carols sound.
*cr* Because to us a Child is born,
  Our Brother, and our King,
*ff* Angels in Heaven, and we on earth,
  Our joyful anthems sing.

# Christmas Carols.

### Carol 60.

*f* Come! ye lof-ty, come! ye low-ly, Let your songs of glad-ness ring;

*p* In a sta-ble lies the Ho-ly, In a man-ger rests the KING.

*cr* See, in Ma-ry's arms re-pos-ing CHRIST by high-est Heaven a-dored;

*f* Come! your cir-cle round Him clos-ing, Pi-ous hearts that love the LORD.

*mf* Come! ye poor, no pomp of station
    Robes the CHILD your hearts adore;
*dim* He, the LORD of all salvation,
    Shares your want, is weak and poor.
*p*  Oxen round about, behold them,
    Rafters naked, cold, and bare!
*cr* See the Shepherds! GOD has told them
    That the PRINCE of Life lies there.


*mf* Come! ye children, blithe and merry,
    This one CHILD your model make;
Christmas holly, leaf, and berry,
    All be prized for His dear Sake.
*cr* Come! ye gentle hearts and tender,
    Come! ye spirits keen and bold,
All in all your homage render,
    Weak and mighty, young and old.


*mf* High above a Star is shining,
    And the Wise Men haste from far;
Come, glad hearts and spirits pining,
    For you all has risen a Star.
*cr* Let us bring our poor oblations,
    Thanks, and love, and faith, and praise;
Come, ye people, come, ye nations,
    All in all draw nigh to gaze!


*f*  Hark! the Heaven of heavens is ringing,
    CHRIST the LORD to man is born;
Are not all our hearts, too, singing
    Welcome, welcome, Christmas Morn?
Still the CHILD, all power possessing,
    Smiles as through the ages past;
*dim* And the song of Christmas blessing
*p*   Sweetly sinks to rest at last.

# Christmas Carols.

Carol 61.

*mf* The shining heralds from on high
　　The joyful tidings bear,
　With acclamations down the sky;
　　And humble shepherds hear.
　　　　Ye people, &c.


*f*　Glory to God, (*pp*) and peace to men,
*f*　　The Heavenly chorus sing;
　Let earth repeat the sound again,
　　To hail the new-born KING.
　　　　Ye people, &c.


*mf* Hosanna! let all earth and Heaven
　　Salute this happy Morn;
　To-day the promised CHILD is given,
　　To us a SON is born.
　　　　Ye people, &c.

# Christmas Carols.

Carol 62.

*p* At midnight, from a Virgin's womb,
    JESUS, our BROTHER evermore,
*cr* Cometh, like bright and Morning Star,
    His kindling rays o'er earth to pour.
    But who could credit this, to-day,
*f* That all the worlds, and all the worlds,
    And all the worlds are His for aye?

*p* In lowly stable is His throne,
    And ox and ass His courtier band,
    His couch, a bed of straw and reed;
    This is the home in Judah's land,
    Which JESUS CHRIST doth choose to-day.
*cr* Though all the worlds, and all the worlds,
*f* And all the worlds are His for aye.

*pp* Hence, lofty pride! your GOD behold,
    Lowly and meek, in garments sad,
    Th' Eternal made a CHILD of Time,
    Almightiness with weakness clad,
    A vesture which He takes to-day;
*cr* While all the worlds, and all the worlds,
*f* And all the worlds are His for aye.

*mf* Ye Shepherds, come with gladsome step,
    Your GOD and SAVIOUR to adore;
    He doth the poor and lowly seek,
    Cherish and love for evermore;
*p* For He is weak and poor to-day,
*cr* Though all the worlds, and all the worlds,
*f* And all the worlds are His for aye!

*f* Noel, Noel, in this sweet feast,
    Noel, Noel, with joy we sing,
    Noel, Noel, to CHRIST the LORD,
    Noel, to CHRIST, our SAVIOUR KING.
*cr* Noel we sing aloud to-day
    Through all the world, and all the world,
*ff* For all the worlds are His for aye!

*This Carol should be sung antiphonally, first and last verse full.*

# Christmas Carols.

**Carol 63.**

1. *mf* Hark! what mean those thrilling voices, Strange-ly sound-ing in the skies; There th' an-gel-ic host re-joic-es, *cr* There those Al - - le-lu - ias rise; Lo! they sing a won-drous sto-ry, Tell-ing of the Sav-iour nigh! Glo-ry in the high-est, Glo-ry; Glo-ry be to God on high.

3. *f* Let us sing the won-drous sto-ry Of our great Re-deem-er's birth, That the bright-ness of His glo-ry Spread and cov - - er all the earth; *cr* Born to reign let all a-dore Him, All cre-a-tion praise its Lord, May we e - ver sing be-fore Him, Glo-ry be to God on high.

# Christmas Carols.

## Carol 64.

*mf* The welcome snow at Christmas-tyde
  Falls shining from the skies:
 On village paths and uplands wide
  All holy-white it lies;
*cr* It crowns with pearl the oaks and pines,
  And glitters on the thorn;
 But purer is the Light that shines
*f*   On gladsome Christmas Morn.


*p* At Christmas-tyde the gracious moon
  Keeps vigil while we sleep,
 And sheds abroad her light's sweet boon,
  On vale and mountain-steep:
 O'er all the slumbering land descends
  Her radiancy unshorn;
*cr* But brighter is the Light, good friends,
*f*   That shines on Christmas Morn.


*p* 'Twas when the world was waxing old,
  And night on Bethlehem lay,
 The Shepherds saw the heavens unfold
  A light beyond the day;
*cr* Such glory ne'er had visited
  A world with sin outworn;
 But yet more glorious Light is shed
*f*   On happy Christmas Morn.


*mf* Those shepherds poor, how blest were they
  The Angels' song to hear!
 In manger cradle as He lay,
  To greet their LORD so dear!
*cr* The LORD of Heaven's Eternal height
  For us a CHILD was born;
 And He, the very Light of light,
*f*   Shone forth that Christmas Morn!


*f* Before His Infant smile afar,
  Were driven the hosts of hell;
 And still in souls that Childlike are
  His guardian Love shall dwell:
*cr* O then rejoice, good Christian men,
  Nor be of heart forlorn;
 December's darkness brings again
*ff*   The Light of Christmas Morn.

# Christmas Carols.

## Carol 65.

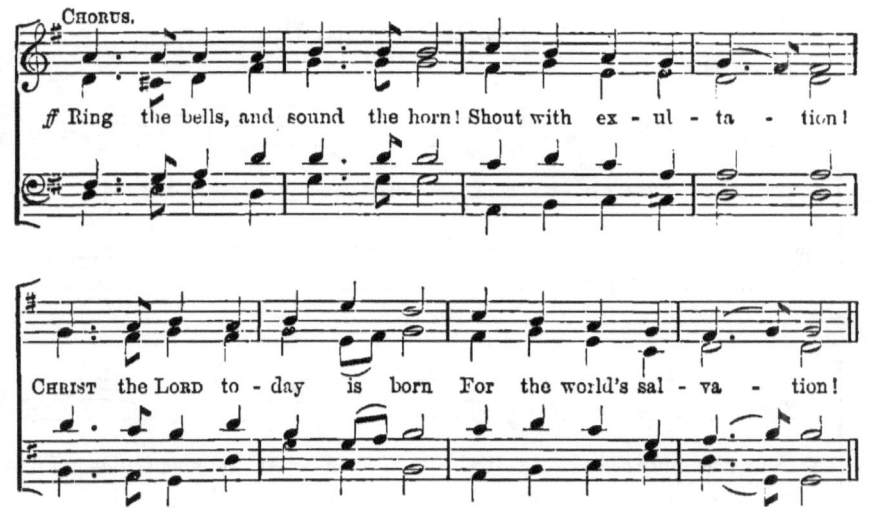

*pp.* All unseen by mortal eye,
    Reverent and lowly ;
    Prostrate there, they laud on High
    Him, the INFANT Holy.
*cr* From their lips celestial rise
    Sounds, with joy o'erflowing,
    Strains upborne beyond the skies,
    Hymns with rapture glowing.
        *ff* Ring the bells, &c.

*mf* Hark the news the Angel tells :—
    Lo ! an INFANT Stranger
*dim* GOD's dear SON among you dwells,
    Born in Bethlehem's manger !
*cr* Bursts a chorus from the sky,
    Loud from Heaven's portal :—
*f*  Glory be to GOD on High,
*pp* Peace, goodwill to mortal !
        *ff* Ring the bells, &c.

*mf* Raphäel, Archangel bright !
    On thine errand wending,
    Forth again into the night
    Mount, the clouds ascending !
    Take of that, thy glittering train,
    Hosts of light, dear Angel !
*dim* Then descend where Bethlehem's plain
    Waits thy longed evangel !
        *ff* Ring the bells, &c.

*mf* Angel spirits earthward led,
    With a hope endearing,
*cr* First to worship, first to spread,
    News of CHRIST's Appearing !
    Trace we out your footfalls light,
    Praise we CHRIST in glory,
*f*  Then waft on the tidings bright
    Of the Gospel story !
        *ff* Ring the bells, &c.

# Christmas Carols.

Carol 66.

*p*   Then in the manger poor, the beast
      Was present with his Lord;
   Then Swains and Pilgrims from the East
      Saw, wondered, and adored.
*cr*  And I this morn would come with them
      This blessed sight to see;
*pp*  And to the Babe of Bethlehem
      Bend low the reverent knee.


*p*   But I have not—it makes me sigh—
      One offering in my power;
   'Tis winter all with me, and I
      Have neither fruit nor flower.
*cr*  O God, O Brother, let me give
      My worthless self to Thee!
*dim* And grant the years which I may live
      May pure and spotless be.


*p*   Grant me Thyself, O Saviour kind,
      Thy Spirit undefiled,
   That I may be in heart and mind
      As gentle as a child;
   That I may tread life's arduous ways
      As Thou Thyself hast trod,
*mf*  And in the might of prayer and praise,
      Keep ever close to God.


*mf* Light of the everlasting Morn,
      Deep through my spirit shine;
   There let Thy Presence newly-born,
      Make all my being Thine:
   There try me as the silver, try
      And cleanse my soul with care,
   Till Thou art able to descry
      Thy faultless Image there.

# Christmas Carols.

Carol 67.

*mf* The bells they seem to utter,—
Ring away all malice,
And each base part
From every heart
In hut or palace!
*cr* And love ye all as brethren;
For CHRIST from Satan's thrall
Was born to-day to save you,
*p* And breathe good-will to all!

*f* The Christmas bells are ringing
Gaily in the steeple;—
For CHRIST's dear sake,
To prayer awake,
All Christian people!
*cr* And joyfully your off'ring
To GOD's fair Altar bring,
And there the Love Eternal
*ff* Of CHRIST your SAVIOUR sing.

Carol 68.

# Christmas Carols.

*p* When the crim-son sun had set Low be-hind the win-try sea,
On the bright And cold midnight *cr* Burst a sound of heaven-ly glee:

*f* Glo — — — — — — — — ri-a in ex-cel-sis De - o,

Glo — — — — — — — — ri-a *ff* in ex-cel-sis De - - o.

*p* Shepherds watching by their fold,
On the crisp and hoary plain,
   In the sky
  *cr* Bright Hosts espy,
Singing in a gladsome strain,
      Gloria, &c.

*p* Where the manger crib is laid,
In the city fair and free,
   Hand in hand,
This Shepherd band
*pp* Worship Christ on bended knee.
      Gloria, &c.

*f* Join with us in welcome song,
Ye who in Christ's Home abide,
   Sing the Love
   Of God above,
Shown at happy Christmas-tide.
  *ff* Gloria, &c.

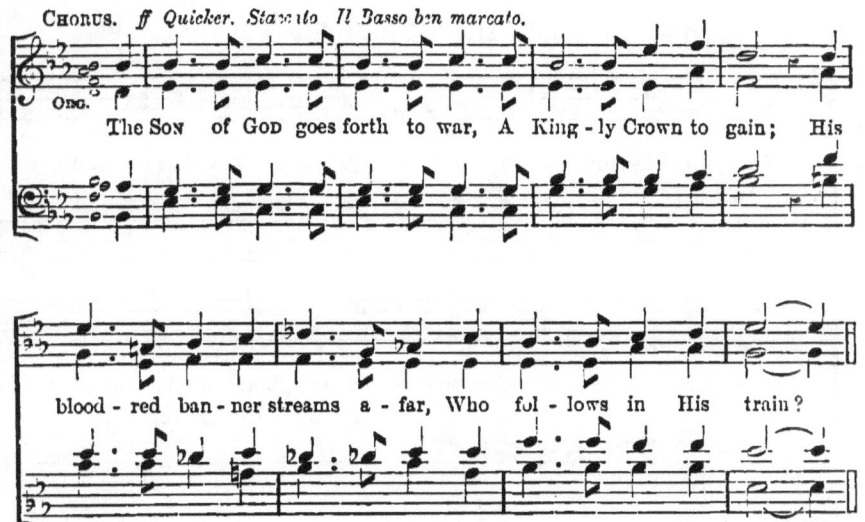

The martyr first, whose eagle eye
  Could pierce beyond the grave,
Who saw his Master in the sky,
  And called on Him to save.
Like Him, with pardon on his tongue
  In midst of mortal pain,
He prayed for them that did the wrong;
  Who follows in his train?
    *ff* The Son of God, &c.

*f* A glorious band, the chosen few
  On whom the SPIRIT came,
Twelve valiant Saints, their hope they knew
  And mocked the Cross and flame.
*dim* They met the tyrant's brandished steel,
  The lion's gory mane,
They bowed their necks, the death to feel:
*cr*  Who follows in their train?
    *ff* The Son of God, &c.

*mf* A noble army, men and boys,
  The matron and the maid,
Around the SAVIOUR'S Throne rejoice,
  In robes of light arrayed.
They climbed the steep ascent of Heaven,
  Through peril, toil, and pain;
O GOD, to us may grace be given
  To follow in their train!
    *ff* The Son of God, &c.

Carol 70. **Saint Stephen.**

*mf* Lord, with what zeal did Thy first mar-tyr breath Thy bless-ed Truth, to such as him with-stood! With what stout mind em-brac-ed he his death, A ho-ly wit-ness seal-ing with his blood! The praise is Thine that him so strong didst make, And blest is he, that died for Thy sake.

*mf* Unquenchèd love in him appeared to be,
When for his murderous foes he did in-treat;
A piercing eye made bright by faith had he;
For he beheld Thee in Thy glory set;
*dim* And so unmoved his patience he did keep,
*pp* He died, as if he had but fallen asleep.

*mf* Our lukewarm hearts with his hot zeal inflame,
So constant, and so loving let us be;
So let us living glorify Thy Name;
*dim* So let us dying fix our eyes on Thee;
And when the sleep of death shall us o'ertake,
*f* With him to Life Eternal us awake!

Carol 71. **Saint John the Evangelist.**

*mf* Teach us by his example, Lord, For whom we honour Thee to-day,
And grant his witness of Thy Word Thy Church enlighten ever may;
And, as beloved, O Christ, he was, And therefore leaned on Thy Breast;
So let us also in Thy grace, And on Thy sacred Bosom rest!

Into us breathe that Life Divine,
  Whose testimony he intends;
About us cause Thy Light to shine,
  That which no darkness comprehends:
And let that Ever Blessed Word
Which all things did create of nought,
Anew create us now, O Lord,
  Whose ruin sin hath almost wrought.

*mf* Thy holy Faith we do profess,
  Us to Thy Fellowship receive;
Our sins we heartily confess,
  Thy Pardon therefore let us have;
*cr* And, as to us Thy Servant gives
  Occasion thus to honour Thee;
So also let our words and lives
  As lights and guides to others be

Carol 72. **The Holy Innocents.**

*mf* That rage whereof the Psalm doth say, "Why are the Gentiles grown so mad?" Appeared in part upon that day, When Herod slain the Infants had; Yet as it saith they stormed in vain; Tho' many Innocents they slew, For Christ they purposed to have slain, Who all their counsels overthrew.

*mf* Thus still vouchsafe Thou to restrain
    The tyrants, Lord, pursuing Thee;
  Thus let our vast desires be slain,
    That Thou mayest living in us be;
*cr* So, whilst we shall enjoy our breath,
    We of Thy Love our songs will frame,
  And with these Innocents, our death
*f*    Shall also glorify Thy Name.

*mf* In type those many died for One;
    That One for many more was slain
  And what they felt in Act alone,
    He did in Will and Act sustain.
Lord, grant that what Thou hast decreed,
    In Will and Act we may fulfil;
And though we reach not to the deed,
    From us, O Lord, accept the Will.

Carol 73. The Holy Innocents.
(FIRST TUNE.)

*mf* The winter sun was setting, The shades of eve were nigh, When loving Jewish mothers Thus sang their lullaby: *dim* O rest thee, gentle baby! The night stars peep; *p* Hush! little birds are silent; *pp* Sleep! dear one, sleep!

*p* The darksome night had fallen;
    There came a ruthless band;
    Each babe on mother's bosom
    Was slain by murderous hand.
*dim* Long rest thee, ransomed baby,
    In slumber deep!
    Within the Arms Eternal
*pp*   Sleep! dear one, sleep!

*p* The morning sun was rising,
    Each mother's heart was torn,
    As o'er her slaughtered infant
    She wailed with grief forlorn:

*dim* God rest thee, murdered baby!
    His blessing keep
    Both babe and mourning mother!
*p*   Sleep! dear one, sleep!

*p* Again the night had fallen;
*cr*   There came a vision bright;
    The babes the LAMB all radiant
    Followed in robes of white.
*f* Joy for my martyr baby!
    No more I weep.
*dim* Till CHRIST shall bid thee follow,
*p*   Sleep! dear one, sleep!

Carol 73. **The Holy Innocents.**
(SECOND TUNE)
*Lento, affettuoso—very slow.*

*mf* The winter sun was setting, The shades of eve were nigh, When loving Jewish mothers Thus sang their lullaby:

O rest thee, gentle baby! The night stars peep! Hush! little birds are silent; Sleep! .... dear one, sleep!

*p* The darksome night had fallen;
There came a ruthless band;
Each babe on mother's bosom
Was slain by murderous hand.
*dim* Long rest thee, ransomed baby,
In slumber deep!
Within the Arms Eternal
*pp* Sleep! dear one, sleep!

*p* The morning sun was rising;
Each mother's heart was torn,
As o'er her slaughtered infant
She wailed with grief forlorn:

*dim* God rest thee, murdered baby!
His blessing keep
Both babe and mourning mother!
*p* Sleep! dear one, sleep!

*p* Again the night had fallen;
*cr* There came a vision bright;
The babes the LAMB all radiant
Followed in robes of white.
*f* Joy for my martyr baby!
No more I weep.
*dim* Till CHRIST shall bid thee follow,
*pp* Sleep! dear one, sleep!

# Circumcision.

**Carol 74.**
*Slow, and not too full. Smoothly.*

    *pp* Sleep, my SAVIOUR, sleep
        On Thy bed of hay,
   *cr* Ere the mourning Angel cometh
        To the moonlit olive garden,
   *f*    Wiping tears away.

    *pp* Sleep, my SAVIOUR, sleep
        Sweet on Mary's breast,
   *cr* Now the Shepherds kneel adoring,
        Now the Mother's heart is joyous,
  *dim* Take a happy rest.

    *pp* Sleep, my SAVIOUR, sleep
        Sweet on Mary's breast.
        Crucified, with wounds and bruises
   *cr* Bleeding, purple, stained, disfigured,
        One day Thou wilt rest.

# Circumcision.

Carol 75.

*p* Sleep, Ho-ly BABE! Up-on Thy .. Mo-ther's breast!
Great LORD of earth, and sea, and sky, How sweet to see Thee calm-ly lie
In such a place of rest! Sleep, Ho-ly BABE!
Thine An-gels watch a-round, All bend-ing low with fold-ed wings,

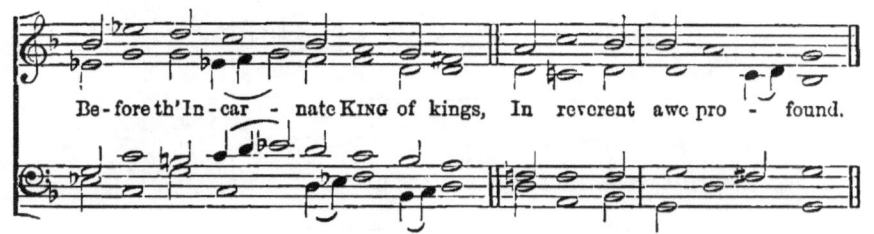

    *p*      Sleep, Holy BABE!
         While I with Mary gaze
       In joy upon that Face awhile,
      Upon the loving Infant smile,
         Which there Divinely plays.
         Sleep, Holy BABE!
*dim*  Ah! take Thy brief Repose:
      Too quickly will Thy Slumbers break,
      And Thou to lengthened pains awake,
*pp*   That death alone shall close.

*pp*     Then must that Brow
         Its thorny crown receive;
      That Cheek, more lovely than the rose,
      Be drenched with blood, and marred with blows,
         That I thereby may live.
         O BABY Blest!
      Sweet JESUS, hear my cry;
      Forgive the wrong that I have done
      To Thee, in causing Thee, GOD'S SON,
         Upon the Cross to die!

*p*      O JESU LORD,
         By Thy sweet Childhood's Years,
      Blot out from their terrific page
      My sins of youth and later age
         In these my contrite tears.
*cr*       So may I sing
         Immortal praise to Thee,
      Who, once a BABE of lowly Birth,
*f*     Now reignest LORD of Heaven and earth,
         In TRINAL UNITY.

# New Year's Eve or Day.

Carol 76.

*mf* Re - mem - ber, life is short, O man, O... man!

Re - mem - ber, O thou man, ere time is spent;

Re - mem - ber, O thou man, how hope seem'd gone,

And how thy God yet called thee to re - pent!

*mf* Remember Adam's fall—O man, O man,
    Remember Adam's fall—too deep to tell!
    Remember Adam's fall, when we were all
    Cast out of Paradise, on earth to dwell.

*mf* Remember God's great Love—O man, O man,
    Remember God's great Love—His Promise made-
    Remember God's great Love—and this the proof,
    He sent His Son our sinful souls to aid.

     *f* The Angels all did sing—O man, O man,
*Unison*   The Angels all did sing, that night so still,
        The Angels all did sing to our great King,
    *p* And Peace proclaim to men of righteous will.

*mf* The Shepherds heard amazed—O man, O man,
    The Shepherds heard amazed, the Angels sing,—
    The Shepherds heard amazed, (*cr*) and joyful praised
*f*  The Blessed Birth of Jesus Christ our King.

*mf* To Bethlehem they did go, O man, O man,
    To Bethlehem they did go, since Christ was there
    To Bethlehem they did go, and found it so,
    Jesus, and Joseph, and His Mother fair.

    *p* As Angels first did say, O man, O man,
*Unison*  As Angels first did say, it came to pass;
       As Angels first did say, the Infant lay
  *pp* In a low Manger-bed, so poor He was.

*p*  In Bethlehem He was born, O man, O man,
    In Bethlehem He was born, that lowly room!
    In Bethlehem He was born, for us forlorn,
    And He did not abhor the Virgin's womb.

*f*  Thanks give to God alway, O man, O man,
    Thanks give to God alway, all purely, wholly;
    Thanks give to God alway, for this glad Day—
*ff* Let all rejoice and hail it,—" Holy, Holy."

\*<sub>\*</sub>\* This Carol may be sung also on the last Sunday after Epiphany.

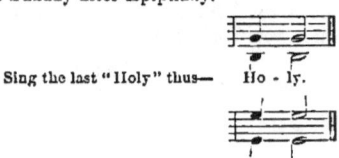

Sing the last "Holy" thus—    Ho - ly.

# New Year's Eve or Day.

Carol 77.
Moderato.

*mf* The moon shone bright and the stars gave light, A little before it was day: Our mighty LORD He looked on us, *or* And bade us awake and pray.

*mf* Awake, awake, good people all,
    Awake, and you shall hear,
The LORD our GOD died on the Cross,
    For us He loved so dear.

*p* O fair, O fair Jerusalem,
    When shall I come to thee?
When shall my sorrows have an end,
    Thy joy when shall I see?

*mf* The fields were green as green could be,
    When from His glorious seat,
Our blessed FATHER watered us,
    With His Heavenly dew so sweet.

*p* And for the saving of our souls
    CHRIST died upon the Cross,
*mf* We ne'er shall show for JESUS CHRIST,
    The love He showed for us.

*mf* The life of man is but a span,
    And cut down in its flower,
We're here to-day, to-morrow gone,
    The creatures of an hour.

*mf* Instruct and teach your children well,
    The while that you are here;
It will be better for your soul,
    When your corpse lies on the bier.

*mf* To-day you be alive and well,
    Worth many a thousand pound;
*p* To-morrow dead and cold as clay,
    Your corpse laid underground.

*mf* With one turf at thine head, O man,
    And another at thy feet;
Thy good deeds and thy bad, O man,
    Will altogether meet.

*mf* [My song is done, I must be gone,
    I stay not longer here;
*f* GOD bless you all, both great and small,
    And send you a glad New Year.]

\*<sub>\*</sub>\* The last verse may be omitted when this Carol is sung in Church.

# Epiphany Carols.

**Carol 78.**
*Allegretto.*

*mf* Gen-tle SAV-IOUR, day and night, Ride three princ-es great in might,
O-ver moun-tain, o-ver plain, Thee a-seek-ing, Thee a-seek-ing,
O-ver moun-tain, o-ver plain, Thee a-seek-ing, gen-tle CHILD.

*mf* Gaspar, Melchior, Bálthăzár,
Those three princes from afar,
Gold and myrrh, and incense bear,
For an offering, for an offering,
To the sweet and gentle CHILD.

*p* Gentle SAVIOUR in the cold,
In the dark with gifts of gold,
Those three princes at the door
Stand a-knocking, stand a-knocking,
Thee to worship, gentle CHILD.

*mf* Enter princes, from the night!
Here, within, is warmth and light,
*cr* JESUS smiles, His hands outspreads
For the offerings, for the offerings,
*f* Praise to Him, the gentle CHILD.

*mf* Joseph, sweep the stable clean,
Strew the straw, though all is mean,
*cr* Here the Temple, here the Throne,
Here the Altar, here the Altar,
*f* Of our KING, this gentle CHILD.

*The third line in each verse is repeated after the fourth.*

# Epiphany Carols.

Carol 79.

*mf* O what joys extatic,
 Thrilled each heart, from far,
When, to guide their footsteps,
 Gleamed that Beacon Star,
O'er that home so holy
 Pouring down its ray,
In His mother's bosom
 Where the INFANT lay !


*p* There no ivory glistens,
 Glows no regal gold,
Nor doth gorgeous purple
 Those fair limbs enfold ;
*dim* But His Court He keepeth
 In a stable bare,
His Throne is a manger
 Rags His purple are.


*mf* Costly pomps and pageants
 Earthly kings array ;
He, a mightier Monarch,
 Hath a nobler sway ;
*p* Straw though be His pallet,
 Mean His garb may be,
*cr* Yet with power transcendent
*f*  He all hearts can free !


*p* At His crib they worship
 Prostrate on the floor ;
And a GOD, there present,
 In that BABE adore ;
*cr* Let us to that INFANT
 We, their offspring true,
Hearts, with faith o'erflowing
*mf*  Give, our tribute due


*mf* Holiest Love presenting
 As gold, to our KING ;
To the Man pure bodies,
 Myrrh-like, chastely bring,
Unto Him, as Incense,
 Vow and prayer address ;
*cr* So with offerings meetest,
 This our GOD confess !


*f* Glory to the FATHER,
 Fount of Light alone ;
Who unto the Gentiles
 Made His Glory known ;
*cr* Equal praise and merit
 Blessed SON, to Thee ;
And to Thee, sweet SPIRIT,
 Evermore shall be !

# Epiphany Carols.

**Carol 80.**

- el, .. *cr* Born is the KING of Is - ra - el.

*mf* They looked up above to the East where a Star
*cr* That beyond them shone out in the Heavens from afar,
And which to the earth did send down a great light,
And so it continued by day and by night.
              *f* Noel, &c.

*mf* And then by the light of that bright guiding Star,
There came three Wise Men from a country afar;
To seek for a KING, it was their intent,
And to follow the Star wherever it went.
              *f* Noel, &c.

*mf* The Star went before them unto the North West,
And seemed o'er the City of Bethlehem to rest,
And there did remain by night and by day,
Right over the place where JESUS CHRIST lay.
              *f* Noel, &c.

*mf* Then entered they all, and those Wise Men three
*dim* Most reverently worshipped with low bended knee;
And offered to CHRIST in His Sacred Presence,
*cr* Gifts of Gold, and of Myrrh, and of sweet Frankincense.
              *f* Noel, &c.

*f* And now Christians all, with most gladsome accord,
*cr* Sing praises, sing praises to JESUS our LORD,
That made both the Heaven, and the Earth out of nought,
And with His Own Blood our Redemption hath wrought.
              *f* Noel, &c.

# Epiphany Carols.

## Carol 81.

*Quickly, and in unison.*

*p* Deep the gloom, and still the night, Dull and drear the wea-ther,

When, the sad night-air de-spite, Met three kings to-ge-ther.

One was old, with snow-white hair, One the prime of man-hood bare,

And the third, a youth, stood there With them on the hea-ther.

*mf* Looking for the promised King,
    Who, in Eastern quarters,
    Soon should spring to life, to rule
    O'er earth's sons and daughters,
    Them this eve, while rapt in sleep,
    One had roused in accents deep,
*cr*  "Haste ye; watch ye; vigil keep
    By Euphrates' waters!"

*mf* In a trice a star shone forth,
*cr*   O! so brightly shining!—
    Nearer, nearer yet it came,
    Still towards earth inclining!
    And 'twas shaped—O! wondrous sight!
    Like a Child enthroned in light,
    Crowned, and with a sceptre bright,
*f*    Victor-cross combining! *

*mf* Up they spring, and quickly hie,
    Each his pathway bending,
*dim*Through the night-born mist and gloom,
    O'er the earth depending.
    How the world in darkness lay,
*cr* Till the Day-Star shed Its ray,
    Nature thus would fain display;—
    Mystic emblems lending.

*mf* Then again the moon her rays
    O'er the earth was streaming;
    Mist and darkness fled apace,
    Stars with light were beaming.
*dim*But yet kneeling 'neath the sky,
    Still the Magi gazed on high,
    As though rapt in ecstacy,
    Or entrancèd dreaming!

*mf* Then the kings with solemn gaze
    Looked on high beholding;
    For the marvel yet to come,
    Heav'n their spirits moulding,
*p*  When behold, with silent awe,
*cr* Suddenly the clouds they saw
    Like a darkened veil withdraw,
*f*   Wonders more unfolding.

*mf* Then one cried, "Behold the Star
    Of which Seers have spoken,
    Beaming on the lands afar,
    And of life the token!
*cr* Haste we, brothers! let us speed;
    See, it moves! It comes to lead
*f*   To the Christ, of Judah's seed
    Born of line unbroken!"

*mf* Up they rise, and bend their way,
    Toil nor labour sparing,
    Over mountain, hill, and plain,
    Costly treasures bearing.—
*cr* So do ye your off'rings make,
    Fear no pain for Jesus' Sake,
    Ever strive Heaven's road to take,
    For your Lord preparing!

---

* An allusion to a legend, preserved in an ancient Commentary on S. Matthew, that the Star, on its first appearance to the Magi, had the form of a radiant child, bearing a sceptre or cross.

# Epiphany Carols.

Carol 82.

*mf* That Blessed Babe, the Holy Child of Love,
    Came down from Heaven that we might reign above;
    The happy news was brought on Angels' wings
    Of our Redemption by the King of kings.
        *f* Then, one and all, &c.


*mf* An earthly wonder not to be denied,
    Born of a Virgin, yet a Heaven-made Bride!
*dim* Not like an earthly prince in pomp and state,
*p*   But poor and mean to make us Heavenly great.
        *f* Then, one and all, &c.


*p*   The night before that happy day of Grace,
    The Blessed Virgin had no resting place;
*pp* But in a manger He, the Lord of Life,
    Was nourished by His Mother, Maid, and Wife.
        *f* Then, one and all, &c.


*mf* Three Wise Men by a Star were thither brought,
    And found the Blessed Babe they long had sought;
    Where, best of spices, and rich costly things,
*cr* They humbly offered to the King of kings.
        *f* Then, one and all, &c.


*f*   With them we worship Christ, come from above,
    The Angels' King, our God, Redeemer, Love—
    At His blest Altar find the Pearl of Price,—
    The Holy Church's Wondrous Sacrifice.
        *ff* Then, one and all, &c.

# Epiphany Carols.

Carol 83.

*mf* Star of Heaven, new glo-ry beam-ing, In the firm-a--ment a-bove Sign from God, to man be-night-ed, Tell-ing of im-mor-tal love! Com-est Thou, in An-gel bright-ness, Is-suing from God's Pa-lace gates,

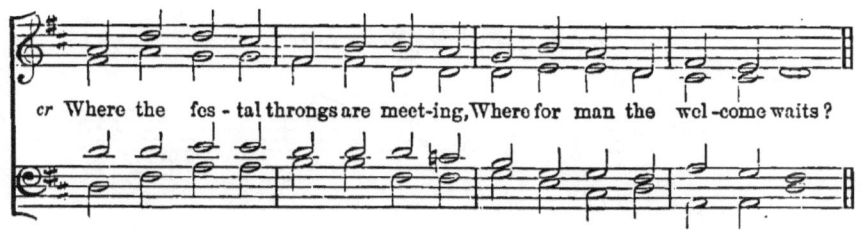

*cr* Where the fes-tal throngs are meeting, Where for man the wel-come waits?

*mf* Star of Heaven, not fixed in splendour
Far above all mortal ken;
But with gentle ray descending
Shining on the paths of men,
Men who yet have Heavenward longings,
And desire their GOD to know;
*cr* Star of Heaven, light now our journey,
Homeward as our footsteps go.


*mf* In the distance of the ages,
Wise Men saw thy cheering ray,
Pointing them to Bethlehem's INFANT,
Guiding by a secret way;
*dim* Midst the tumult of the city,
Thou wast hidden from their sight,
'Parted thence—(*cr*) "O joy exceeding,"
*f*   Once again they see thy light!


*mf* Star of Heaven, still lead our wanderings,
As we watch the Light from GOD,
Streaming calmly, beautifully,
All along our lonely road;
*cr* Till we see the glory standing
Over the abiding place,
Where the LORD Himself is waiting,
*f*   Full of Glory, full of Grace!

# Epiphany Carols.

**Carol 84.**
*Andante.*

*mf* Come, good Christ-ians, join our song, As we pace a hap-py throng, As we pace a hap-py throng, Thro' the gar-den walks so wide, On Mount Car-mel's sun-ny side, Gar-den rich with flow-ers rare, Scent-ing all the sum-mer air.

*mf* Gather, Christian, blossoms gay,
    Gather fruit this gladsome day;
    All bright flowers, my gentle bride,
    On Mount Carmel's sunny side,
    Serve for thine adorning well,
    Mystic lessons while they tell.

*mf* Gather first the sunflower bright,
    Turning ever to the light;
    Stock and wall-flower sweet, that fling
    On the breeze their offering;
    Gather lilies, stainless, pure,
    Everlastings that endure.

*mf* Cull the woodbine that entwines,
    Tulips gay in flaming lines,
    Pansies blue, and primrose pale;
    Gather violets without fail,
    That beneath the leafage hide,
    On Mount Carmel's sunny side.

*mf* Carmel's garden, oh, how fair!
    Countless flowers are blooming there,
    Flowers of varied odour blow,
    Flowers of every lustre glow;
*cr* Lo! the garden we have trod
*f* Surely is the Church of God.

*mf* Here the doctors stand and gaze,
    Clear-eyed on the solar blaze;
    Here the hermits from their rock
    Waft their virtues like the stock;
    Virgins are the lily white,
    Martyrs' wounds the tulip bright.

*p* Humble souls are violets blue,
    Wet with penitential dew;
    Meekness like a primrose lies,
    Constancy nor fades nor dies;
    Broken hearts by heaven dyed,
    Pansies peaceful, satisfied.

*mf* Clinging spirits, that entwine
    Round the cross, are eglantine;
    Here, from out monastic cell,
    Shakes the Canterbury bell;
    Prelates here, a gallant flock,
    Blaze as stately hollyhock.

    There's a fountain, limpid, clean,
    Waters Carmel's garden green,
    Never failing, year by year,
    Opened by the soldier's spear.
*cr* Once he smote the living Rock,
*f* Forth it spouted at the shock.

*Repeat the second line of each verse.*

# Epiphany Carols.

Carol 85.

*mf* Manifest at Jordan's stream,
    Prophet, Priest, and King supreme;
    And at Cana wedding-guest
    In Thy Godhead manifest;
    Manifest in power Divine,
    Changing water into wine;
*f*  Anthems be to Thee addrest,
    God in Man made manifest.

*mf* Manifest in making whole
    Palsied limbs and fainting soul;
    Manifest in valiant fight,
    Quelling all the devil's might;
    Manifest in gracious Will,
    Ever bringing good from ill;
*f*  Anthems be to Thee addrest,
    God in Man made manifest.

    Sun and moon shall darkened be,
    Stars shall fall, the heaven shall flee;
*cr* Christ will then like lightning shine,
    All will see His glorious Sign;
    All will then the trumpet hear,
    All will see the Judge appear;
*f*  Thou by all wilt be confest,
    God in Man made manifest.

*p*  Grant us Grace to see Thee, Lord,
    Mirrored in Thy holy Word;
    May we imitate Thee now,
    And be pure, as pure art Thou;
    That we like to Thee may be
    At Thy great Epiphany;
*f*  And may praise Thee, ever Blest,
    God in Man made manifest.

# Epiphany Carols.

Carol 86.

*mf* From the East-ern moun-tains Press-ing on they come,
Wise Men in their wis-dom *p* To His hum-ble Home.
Stirred by deep de-vo-tion Hast-ing from a-far,
Ev-er jour-ney-ing on- - -ward, *f* Guid-ed by a Star.

*p*   There their Lord and Saviour
      Meek and lowly lay,
    Wondrous Light that led them
      Onward on their way ;
*cr*  Ever now to lighten
      Nations from afar,
    As they journey Homeward
*f*     By that guiding Star.


*p*   Thou Who in a manger
      Once hast lowly lain,
*f*    Who dost now in glory
      O'er all kingdoms reign,
*mf* Gather in the heathen
      Who in lands afar
    Ne'er have seen the brightness
      Of Thy guiding Star.

*mf* Gather in the outcasts,
      All who go astray,
    Throw Thy Radiance o'er them,
      Guide them on their way,
    Those who never knew Thee,
      Those who wander far,
    Guide them by the brightness
      Of Thy guiding Star.

*mf* Onward through the darkness
      Of the lonely night,
    Shining still before them
      With Thy kindly Light.
    Guide them, Jew and Gentile,
      Homeward from afar,
    Young and old together,
      By Thy guiding Star.

*mf* Until every nation,
      Whether bond or free,
    'Neath Thy Starlit-Banner,
      Jesu, follows Thee
*cr*  O'er the distant mountains,
      To that Heavenly Home,
    Where nor sin nor sorrow
*f*     Evermore shall come.

# Epiphany Carols.

Carol 87.
*Brightly.*

*mf* To Adam's sons, an exiled race,
    Their GOD Himself, with wondrous Grace,
      Hath come and sought to them
    Who sought Him not; and they surprised
*cr*  Behold a light that leads to CHRIST,—
      The Star of Bethlehem.
*ff*  Alleluia, Alleluia, Alleluia, Praise ye the LORD!

*mf* Clear from the Heavens a Ray of Love
    Stood over Mary's house, and wove
      A dazzling diadem!
*cr*  Ring out your joy, all Christians true,
    And may CHRIST's Light be seen by you,—
      His Star of Bethlehem.
*ff*  Alleluia, Alleluia, Alleluia, Praise ye the LORD!

*mf* Man is no lonely wanderer now
    Since on the INFANT JESUS' Brow
      First shone that peaceful beam;
*p*   One with us in our low estate,
*cr*  He lifts our heart to Heaven's high Gate!
      Hail, Star of Bethlehem!
*ff*  Alleluia, Alleluia, Alleluia, Praise ye the LORD!

# Epiphany Carols.

Carol 88.

Full. How blest with more than woman's bliss was she the espoused Maid, And Virgin Mother when she saw upon her bosom laid . . Her newborn BABE, and gaz'd on Him with meek adoring eye, *cr* with meek adoring eye, . . with meek adoring oye, . . Be-

-neath the Ho - LY SPI - RIT's Light, *f* the power of GOD Most High!

*Dec. mf* Methinks I see thee, Mary, look on Him with fixed gaze,
    And ponder in thy secret heart the Almighty FATHER's ways,
    As to thy thoughts in contrast strong the past and present rise,
  *f* The glory whence thy INFANT came, (*p*) the stable where He lies!

*Can. mf* Fit birth for Him, Who, when with GOD and man in favour grown,
    His FATHER's glory shall display,—His FATHER's and His Own;
    When at His Will the crystal stream to generous wine shall turn,
  *f* And from His Lips the astonished poor GOD's glorious Gospel learn:—

*Full mf* When the blind eye unclosed shall see its great Restorer near,
  *cr* And the dumb tongue His Praise proclaim, and the deaf ear shall hear,
    The leprous taint be cleansed, and death beneath His Feet be trod,
  *f* And subject fiends their prey release, and own the SON of GOD.

*Dec. mf* O Mary, Virgin Mother blest, what rapture shall be thine,
    Thus in thy CHILD to see fulfilled each Heaven-appointed sign;
  *p* Although a sword thy bosom pierce amid the mighty throes,
  *cr* While o'er thy loved, thy worshipped SON, the glooms sepulchral close,

*Can. mf* Thy heart shall joy to know that He, the OFFSPRING of thy womb,
  *cr* Thy SAVIOUR, Mary, and thy LORD, hath burst the rock-hewn tomb,
    And soared His Heritage to claim high o'er the realms of light,
  *f* The Bosom of His FATHER's love the Right Hand of His Might.

*Full pp* But hold! thy INFANT sleeps, and there, beside the Holy CHILD,
    Take thou thy slumber, Maiden meek, blest Mother undefiled:
    Sleep thou, while Angels wake around, and conscious Whom they tend
    With folded wings and shaded eyes in sign of worship bend!

# Epiphany Carols.

**Carol 89.**

*mf* To earth from Heaven glad tidings I unfold, The Angel *cr* cries, Christ Lord of world is born In *f* Bethlehem Judah, as the Seers foretold, This hallowed Morn.

*mf* Him do the joyful Choir of Angels sing,
　　The Star declares ; Him Eastern Princes greet,
And mystic gifts in adoration bring,
　　　　Oblations meet ;

*mf* Incense to God, and Myrrh to grace His Tomb,
　　For tribute to their King, a golden store ;
*cr* One they revere, three with three offerings come
　　　*f* And Three adore !

*f* All glory to the One yet Triune Lord,
　　To God and to His Royal Offspring give ;
So to the Spirit, Which of Both outpoured,
　　　　True hearts receive.

## Epiphany Carols.

**Carol 90.** *Smoothly.*

mf Look up (look up) to Heav'n (to Heav'n), lo! stars (lo, stars) are there; The ho-ly patriarch gazed on high *cr* And choirs of light, se-rene and fair *f* All sang for him a pro-phe-cy,—

"That God would all men bless by One,
Who should be born of Abraham's race;"
And Abraham saw from far His Son,
Full of immortal Truth and Grace.
Then clouds rolled on and hid the light,
And there was darkness overhead.
"Is there no Star to cheer the night?"—
"I see it not,"—the Prophet said,
"But there will rise o'er Judah's land
A light I shall behold from far!"
While still in solitude shall stand
Balaam, although he sees the Star!

Who are the wise? the pure in heart?
For them the Star of God appears;
*cr* For them the clouds asunder part,
*f* And mists dissolve, and darkness clears.
*f* They hail the Light on Bethlehem's crest,
They watch the Glory slanting down;
It settles o'er the Virgin's breast,
Shining the Heaven-born Jesus' crown.
*f* O "God with us!"—all joy restored;
No "Tidings good" for man but this!
Henceforth we know no absent Lord,
His presence is perpetual bliss.
*f* The Lord our Everlasting Light,
And all our days of mourning done!
Now pass away, ye clouds and night!—
*ff* Praise we the Father, Spirit, Son!

# Epiphany Carols.

## Carol 91.

# Epiphany Carols.

**Carol 92.**
*Smoothly.*

*mf* O love-ly .. Voic-es of ... the sky, That hymned the Sav-iour's Birth, Are ye not sing-ing still .. on High, *p* Who once sang Peace on Earth? *mf* Still o'er us float those ho-ly strains, Where-with in days gone by *cr* Ye blessed the

low - ly Sy - rian Swains, *f* O Voic-es of the sky!

    *mf* O clear and shining Light, whose beams
        A heavenly radiance shed
        Around the palms, and o'er the streams,
        And on the Shepherds' head,—
        Be near through life, be near in death,
        As in that holiest night
*cr* Of hope, of gladness, and of faith,
*f*     O clear and shining Light!

    *mf* O Star, which ledd'st to Him Whose Love
        Brought down man's ransom free,
        Thou still art midst the hosts above,
        We still may gaze on thee!
*cr* In Heaven thy light doth never set,
        Thy rays earth may not dim;
        O, send them forth to guide us yet,
*f*     Bright Star which led to Him!

# Epiphany Carols.

Carol 93.

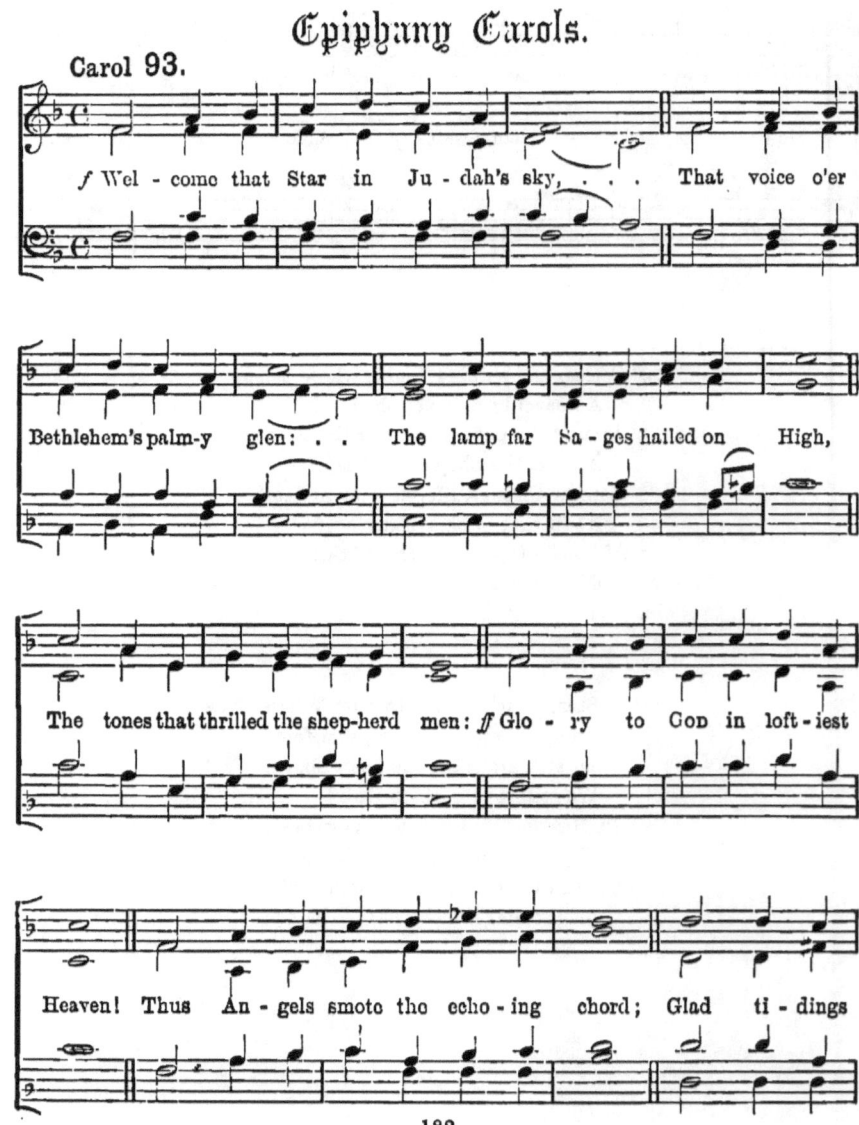

 *mf* The Shepherds sought that Birth Divine,
   The Wise Men traced their guided way;
   There, by strange light and mystic sign,
   The God they came to worship lay.
*dim* A human BABE in beauty smiled,
   Where lowing oxen round Him trod :
*pp* A Maiden clasped her awful CHILD,
   Pure Offspring of the Breath of God.


 *p* Those voices from on high are mute,
   The Star the Wise Men saw is dim :
 *cr* But hope still guides the wanderer's foot,
   And Faith renews the Angel **hymn** :
 *ff* Glory to God in loftiest **Heaven** !
   Touch with glad **hand** the ancient chord,
   Good Tidings **unto** man forgiven,
 *p*  Peace **from the** Presence of the LORD.

# Epiphany Carols.

**Carol 94.**

*mf* That so Thy bless-ed Birth, O CHRIST, Might thro' the world be spread a-bout,
The Star ap-pear-ed in the East, Where-by the Gen-tiles found Thee out;
And offered Thee Myrrh, In-cense, Gold, Thy three-fold Of-fice to un-fold.

*mf* Sweet JESUS, let that Star of Thine,
    Thy Grace, which guides to find out Thee,
    Within our hearts for ever shine,
    That Thou of us found out mayest be;
*cr*     And Thou shalt be our KING therefore,
*f*     Our PRIEST and PROPHET Evermore!

*mf* Tears that from true repentance drop,
    Instead of myrrh, present will we:
*cr* For Incense we will offer up
    Our prayers and praises unto Thee;
    And bring for gold each pious deed,
    Which doth from saving faith proceed.

*mf* And as those Wise Men never wen
    To visit Herod any more;
    So, finding Thee, we will repent
    Our courses followed heretofore;
    And that we homeward may retire
    The way by Thee we will enquire.

# Epiphany Carols.

### Carol 95.

*mf* The stars shone brightly over-head,
*p*  The air was calm and still,
*cr* O'er Bethlehem fields its rays were shed,
 The dew lay on the hill:
*mf* We see no throne, no palace fair,
 Where is the KING? O where? O where?

*pp* An old man knelt at a manger low,
 A babe lay in a stall;
 The starlight played on the Infant brow,
 Deep silence lay o'er all:
 A maiden bent o'er the BABE in prayer:—
*ff* There is the KING, O there! O there!

# Epiphany Carols.

**Carol 96.**

Chorus. Full. Allegro moderato.

*ff* Noel, Noel, Noel, Born is the King of Israel.

Verse. Solo.

*mf* O Child of wonder! Child of love! Good Angels hasting from above, Did guard Thee safe from Herod's hand, And convoy Thee to Egypt's land.

*ff* Noel, Noel, Noel, Born is the King of Israel.
*mf* To Egypt's land our Lord was brought
When Judah's King His life had sought,
There God full soon a work had done,
And then from Egypt called His Son.

*ff* Noel, Noel, Noel, Born is the King of Israel.
*mf* For what had Egypt known like this,
Marvel of Heliopolis—
*cr* When prostrate idols fell before
*f* Christ coming to their temple floor!

*ff* Noel, Noel, Noel, Born is the King of Israel.
But O what mightier deed is told,
*mf* When God, the Child of twelve years old,
To His own Temple's dread surprise
Cast down the wisdom of the wise?

*ff* Noel, Noel, Noel, Born is the King of Israel.
*mf* O Child of Bethlehem! man's delight;
*cr* O Glorious Child of Egypt's flight;
O Child, Who in the Temple stood,
*ff* We praise Thee, Wisdom of our God!

# Epiphany Carols.

**Carol 97.**

*mf* When CHRIST was born of pure Ma-rie, In Beth-le-hem, that fair ci-tie, The An-gels sang with mirth and glee, *f* In Ex-cel-sis Glo-ri-a, In Ex-cel-sis Glo-ri-a.

*mf* Herdmen beheld those Angels bright,
To them appeared they with great light,
And said GOD'S SON is born this night,—
 *f* In Excelsis Gloria

*mf* This KING is come to save mankind,
In Scripture promised as we find,
Therefore this Song have we in mind,—
 *f* In Excelsis Gloria.

*p*  Grant us, O LORD, for Thy great Grace,
  In heaven the bliss to see Thy Face,
*cr* Where we may sing to Thy solace,—
 *f* In Excelsis Gloria.

# Epiphany Carols.

Carol 98.

*f* Thou art our God, we ex-alt Thee, we praise Thee, Faithful and true are Thy Counsels of old: Hymns of thanksgiving Thy People shall raise Thee, Hailing the mercy Thy Prophets foretold.

*ff* Bright is Thy Coming, and tempests, long hovering
　Over our world, are dispersed by Thy Grace;
　Thou shalt destroy all the face of the covering,
　Mantling the sinful, and hiding the base.

*f* This is the joy that enkindles our praises,
　This the glad song of Creation's New Birth:
　GOD shall wipe sorrows and tears from all faces,
　GOD shall give Paradise back to our earth.

*f* This is our GOD, lo, for Him we have waited, [save:
　This is the LORD, and He cometh to
　Joy for the world that His Mercy created,
　Triumph o'er sin, and o'er death and the grave.

*f* Thou art our GOD, and we praise Thee, we bless Thee,
　Wonderful things our Redeemer hath done;
*cr* Great is Thy Power and Thy Love, we confess THEE,
*f* 　FATHER and SPIRIT and Well-beloved SON.

# Epiphany Carols.

### Carol 99.

*mf* Brightest and best of the sons of the morning, Dawn on our darkness and lend us thine aid! *cr* Star of the East, the horizon adorning, Guide where our Infant Redeemer is laid.

*p* Cold on His Cradle the dewdrops are shining,
　　Low lies His Head with the beast of the stall;
*cr* Angels adore Him in slumber reclining,
　　Maker, and Monarch, and Saviour of all!

*mf* Say, shall we yield Him, in costly devotion,
　　Odours of Edom and offerings Divine;
Gems of the mountain and pearls of the ocean,
　　Myrrh from the forest and gold from the mine?

*mf* Vainly we offer each ample oblation,
　　Vainly with gifts would His Favour secure;
*cr* Richer by far is the heart's adoration,
　　Dearer to God are the prayers of the poor!

# Epiphany Carols.

**Carol 100.** *Slow.*

*p* Knowing not the great CRE-A-TOR Lay the world in deepest night,
*cr* When there broke on Eastern mountains Wondrous-ly a gold-en light.
*mf* And the grace-star led the Ma-gi *p* To the low-ly cat-tle stall *cr* Whence the glo-ry dai-ly widening *f* Brought Redemption to us all.

*mf* Prostrate fall the bloody altars,
    Men to bats their idols fling,
*cr* And the Gospel reigns triumphant
    To the Ocean's widest ring.

And where its bright beams are burning
    Rises up an Empire new,
On the ruins of old temples
*f*     Pleads the Offering one and true.

# Epiphany Carols.

### Carol 101.

*mf* As with gladness men of old
Did the guiding Star behold;
*cr* As with joy they hailed its light,
Leading onward, beaming bright;
*p* So, most gracious Lord, may we
*cr* Evermore be led to Thee.

As with joyful steps they sped,
Saviour, to Thy lowly bed,
There to bend the knee before
Him Whom heaven and earth adore;
So may we with willing feet
Ever seek Thy mercy-seat.

As they offered gifts most rare
At Thy cradle rude and bare;
So may we with holy joy,
Pure and free from sin's alloy,
All our costliest treasures bring,
Christ, to Thee, our heavenly King.

*mf* Holy Jesus! every day
Keep us in the narrow way;
And, when earthly things are past,
Bring our ransomed souls at last
Where they need no star to guide,
*cr* Where no clouds Thy glory hide.

*mf* In the heavenly country bright
Need they no created light;
Thou its Light, its Joy, its Crown,
Thou its Sun which goes not down;
*ff* There for ever may we sing
*cr* Alleluias to our King.

# Epiphany Carols.

Carol 102.

*p*  We plead for the fallen, Thy mercy we seek,
    For those who have left Thee, fainthearted and weak,
    O give us more patience, more hope, and more faith,
    To hold fast Thy promise through sorrow and death.

*mf*  By Thy blessed descending, Thy glorious birth,
*p*  Thy sorrows and suffering, Thy life upon earth,
*pp*  By Thy parting words spoken, Thy last awful sigh,
*f*  By Thy bright resurrection, Thy dwelling on high;

*mf*  We pray Thee to hear us, to pardon and save,
    And for our soul's cleansing to trouble the wave.
    Thy Church is in sorrow, in danger and fear—
    O stretch forth Thy hand, for the breakers are near.

*mf*  Once more send the message the shepherds heard then—
*p*  Be peace on the earth, and good will unto men.
*cr*  May a new star shine o'er us, a new life begin,
    A new era dawning from sorrow and sin.

*mf*  Poor, sinful, and weak, with no power of our own,
    We trust in Thy mercy, in Thee, Thee alone,
    We ever confide in Thy wonderful love,
    That brought Thee to suffer, from glory above.

*f*  We praise Thee, we bless Thee, we glorify Thee,
    We praise the Eternal, the glorious THREE;
    While Angels announce the Immaculate Birth,
    O hear our weak praises, the voices of earth.

*See Treble Part, Edition E or F, for division of words.*

# Epiphany Carols.

Carol 103.

-cense, and death-ly myrrh, their precious tribute bring.

*f* Hail, JESU, KING of kings, to Thee no bauble crown,
But all our hearts' best gold we bring, and at Thy feet cast down,
  *mf* Thee, Incarnate GOD, we sing,
  Thee the Sages worshipping
*cr* Regal gold, and priestly frankincense, and deathly myrrh, their mystic symbols bring.


*mf* Lo! sweet memorial of Thy atoning Love
Thy servants offer here on earth, as Thou in Heaven above.
  Thee, Eternal PRIEST, we sing,
  Thee the Sages worshipping
*cr* Regal gold, and priestly frankincense, and deathly myrrh, their mystic symbols bring.


*pp* Hail, SON of MAN, in all our conflicts here below
Remember us, for Thou hast felt the pangs of mortal woe.
  *p* Thee, Very MAN, we sing,
  Thee the Sages worshipping
*cr* Regal gold, and priestly frankincense, and deathly myrrh, their mystic symbols bring.

# Epiphany Carols.

**Carol 104.**

*mf* Now, hither come to me,
    Priest, scribe, Essene ascetic,
  And search ye out, and see
    In mystic scroll prophetic,
      In what blest place fair-famed,
      The seers have long proclaimed
*f*   Messiah born must be!


*mf* Fair Bethlehem, goodly town!
    There shall the Princely Stranger,
*dim*Coming from Zion down,
*p*    Be born in lowly manger!
    *mf* Trembled the King this hearing,
      A mighty peril fearing
  To his own royal crown.


*mf* Now pass the wide gate through,
    And haste for love and pity,
  And search with vigour due
    For CHRIST, in David's city!
    *cr*  Return ye then, and lead me,
      That I may thither speed me,
*f*  And worship Him with you!


*mf* Ah! Herod, King, refrain
    'Gainst CHRIST so fondly scheming!
  With guileful craft in vain
    Of impious crime thou'rt dreaming!
      Him shall thine eyes see never,
    *cr*  Till He shall come, for ever,
*f*  O'er every foe to reign!

# Epiphany Carols.

**Carol 105.**

*p* No purple here is seen, no pomp of splendour,
    Rude swaddling bands enfold each sacred Limb,
    Yet shepherds kneel, (*cr*) their silent praise to render,
*f* And Seraphs wondering, chant their carol-hymn.

*mf* The gentle stars in solemn courses wending,
    Throw their soft lustre o'er the manger-shed,
    With JESUS' sleeping smile their radiance blending,
*cr* Till one bright halo circles round His Head.

4. *p* Angels with folded wing, and breath abated,
    Gaze tremblingly upon that Little ONE,
    Muse on their GOD'S Great Glory Incarnated,
   *cr* And worship JESUS, GOD and Mary's Son.

5. *p* Earth does not heed, (*f*) though Heaven itself rejoices,
    While myriads swell the "Gloria" sung on High,
*dim* No echo can they find 'mid earthly voices,
*p*    Save Mary, singing her sweet lullaby;—

6. *p* Mary, and those who love with her to ponder
    On mysteries half-seen, yet half-concealed,
    Longing to know—yet willing still to wonder,
    Waiting in faith, till all shall be revealed.

*mf* Such souls alone can contemplate the Glory,
*cr*   Which, darkling, breaks upon their eager sight,
    True hearts which own the Incarnation story,
    Need ask no greater sign,—no clearer light.

*mf* They muse in Faith,— and He in Mercy shineth,
*p*    They gaze in silence,—(*cr*) and the darkness flies;
*dim* "EMMANUEL" on Mary's heart reclineth,
*p*    He sleeps,—(*ff*) He wakes,—Behold the Day-Star rise!

---

\* When, as in verses 4, 5, and 6, the first syllable is accented, the first crotchet should be omitted, and the voices come in on the first beat of the bar. A little care in the division of syllables will make every line run smoothly. See Edition E or F.

# Epiphany Carols.

**Carol 106.**
*Moderato. Firmly.*

*mf* O! come ye down to Cana, And Christ's dear foot-prints trace,

For He is gone with Mary, A marriage feast to grace.

How fair the happy concourse! How bright the gay robes shine!

*cr* How joyous, too, the feasters! *dim* But lo! there lacketh wine!

*mf* Soft speaks the kindly JESUS
    To servants standing by :
Now fill these pots with water,
    Which here all empty lie ;
And bear ye to the ruler.
    'Tis done at JESUS' sign,
*cr* And lo ! the water limpid
*f*    Is changed to ripe red wine !


*mf* Then knowing not the marvel
    Was wrought by JESUS' Word,
The ruler to the bridegroom
    Saith, with amazement stirred :
All men at the beginning
    Their best wine give, but Thou
*cr* The richest, noblest, sweetest,
*f*    Hast kept back until now !


*mf* O ! come ye down to Cana !
    For lo ! whate'er betide,
*cr* The Bridegroom now is JESUS,
    The Church, His holy bride !
*f* And He the living streamlet
    From GOD's bright throne above,
Doth give as cheering wine-drops
    In chalice of His Love !

### Carol 107. Epiphany Carols.

*mf* So-jour-ners and stran-gers, Seek-ing our true home,
Meet-ing with rough dan-gers, As we on-ward roam:
Strength is oft-en fail-ing, On des-truc-tion's brink,—
Lord, Thy Power pre-vail-ing Will not let us sink.

*mf* Troubles are molesting,
But if Thou be near,
On Thy succour resting,
We shall have no fear.
Lord Almighty, knowing
All our feebleness,
Grace from Thee o'erflowing,
Comforts our distress.

*p* Now the shadows lengthen,
And we count the hours,
Near the end, O strengthen
Our fast-failing powers;
*cr* Thy right hand extending!—
All on Thee we cast,
So, Thy love befriending,
*f* Gain our home at last.

# Epiphany Carols.

**Carol 108.**
*Smoothly.*

*mf* O sing of the Saviour's might, *cr* Sing all through the live-long day; *f* For now He grants the Heavenly Light Which leads to Him the Way.

*mf* O muse on His Holy Word,
    Revealed by His Love for you—
The Truth which is by all adored,
*f*     To Whom is homage due.

*f* O give we our hearts to Him,
    Who brought us from God rich store,
And died upon the Cross for sin,
    Our Life for Evermore.

# Conversion of Saint Paul.

**Carol 109.**
*Lightly.*

*mf* Earn-est-heart-ed Saul, O why, Breath-ing threats so ruth-less-ly, Bear-ing slaugh-ter and the sword, Per-se-cut-est thou the LORD?

*p* Why, with zeal that ne-ver faints, Per-se-cut-est thou the Saints?

*mf* Old Damascus' gates within
Peered the wolf of Benjamin,
Hasting, brooking no delay,
Eager to devour the prey.
*cr* Rise, O LORD, avert the shock,
Seize the wolf, protect the flock.

*mf* Fear not, little flock, but pray;
JESUS may the tyrant stay,
May the smiter smite with grace,
May make fiercest foes embrace.
*p* Darkness now may fill your home,
But (*f*) "arise, thy light is come."

Gen. xlix. 27

*mf* Up within the city-wall
*cr* Springs the cry from Christians all;
Jesu, Shepherd of the sheep,
From this Saul Thy servants keep!
*f* Lo! He hears the voices there,
Grants the Proto-martyr's prayer.


*mf* Light, upon that darkened mind,
Set Saul free, who came to bind:
Light of more than earthly day,
Light beyond the noon-tide ray.
Though thine eyes are sealed in gloom,
*f* See, for thy Light too is come.


*mf* Lightened by that heavenly glare,
Spirit-taught in vision rare
Things unknown to mortal view,
Paul now builds, what Saul o'erthrew.
*p* Chastened zeal and humbled pride
Bow before the Crucified.


*mf* Manifest Thyself, O Lord,
Teach us by the Apostle's word;
His conversion ever be
An Epiphany of Thee,
*cr* Showing, by Thy Holy Rood,
*f* Grace triumphant, sin subdued.


*mf* Oh! if, in these latter days,
Darkened faith and languid praise,
Counting zeal a foolish thing,
Cause a costless offering;
*cr* Flash across our perilous night;
*f* "In Thy Light, shall we see Light."


*mf* And if strife, engendering strife,
Tear and soil our better life;
*dim* Jesu, Lord, Thy Spirit send,
Zeal with Charity to blend.
*cr* When loved error clouds the sight,
Speak the word, (*ff*) "Let there be Light."

# Purification of the Blessed Virgin Mary.
**Carol 110.**

*mf* Blessèd, for thou barest
    Jesus in thy womb;
Blessèd from the manger,
    Onwards to the tomb,
And since thou returnedst
    To Saint John's abode;—
*cr* All shall call thee blessèd,
    Mother of our God.

*mf* Thinking how the glory,
    Of the Highest, sat
Overshadowing Mary,
    Our Magnificat
*dim* Echoes hers, as meekly
    From her voice it flowed;
*cr* All shall call thee blessèd,
    Mother of our God.

*mf* Hath not God Almighty
    Done for thee great things?
Making thee the mother
    Of the King of kings?
*p* Thou the first to know Him,
    Veiled in flesh and blood!—
*cr* All shall call thee blessèd,
    Mother of our God.

*mf* Yet a higher glory,
    Yet a fairer crown,
Shines for ever o'er thee,
    Than that sweet renown.
For thou wast obedient
    To the heavenly word!—
*cr* All shall call thee blessèd,
    Mother of our Lord.

*mf* But Thy praise, O Jesus,
    Loftier songs employ;
*cr* Hearts for Thee exulting,
    Leap within for joy;
*f* Joy, that God the Father
    Sent Thee from above;
Joy for the o'ershadowing
    Of the Spirit's Love.

# Purification of the Blessed Virgin Mary.

### Carol 111.

*mf* The LORD is with thee, blessed Maid,
  The LORD shall be thy CHILD,
 Behold Thy handmaid, Mary said,
  To bear the UNDEFILED.
*cr* And all shall hail the joy for thee,
  *f* Praise FATHER, &c.


*mf* What joy to Mary, Mother-Maid,
  Beneath o'er-shadowing GOD;
 All joy, for while she knelt and prayed,
  CHRIST came to her abode!
 And all shall hail the joy for thee,
  *f* Praise FATHER, &c.


*mf* What joy and mystery, Mary, Maid,
  Touched thee with mingled smart,
 When in the Temple Simeon said,
  A sword shall pierce thy heart,
 And all shall watch that mystery,
  *f* Praise FATHER &c.


*pp* What grief of Heaven, O Mary, Maid,
  To see thy SON despised
 More than thyself, when scoffers said
  Their taunts, all undisguised;
*cr* And yet that sorrow brings our joy.
  *f* Praise FATHER, &c.


*p* How Angels watched thee, Mary, Maid,
  And soothed thee in thy loss!
 And Gabriel, not in light arrayed,
  Yet near thee at the Cross:
*cr* And all shall hail that mystery!
  *f* Praise FATHER, &c.

# Purification of the Blessed Virgin Mary.

**Carol 112.**

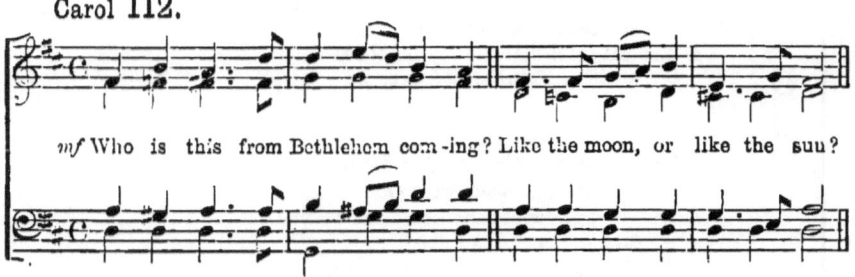

*mf* Who is this from Bethlehem com-ing? Like the moon, or like the sun?

Thou, O Christ, our flesh as-sum-ing, Thou the Vir-gin's Ho-ly One!

*p* Lo! with Thee, the mo-ther kneels, In Thy House the law o-beys,

 *mf* Suddenly, O KING immortal,
  As Thy Prophets had foretold,
 *cr* Thou hast passed the sacred portal,
  Where Thy glory dwelt of old:
*f* Temple, priest, and altar now,
  All in Thee are purified;
 Splendour of all worship, Thou
  Wilt with all Thy Saints abide.
  *ff* Glory to the FATHER, SON,
  And the SPIRIT, THREE in ONE.

# EXTRACTS FROM REVIEWS.

"We welcome with great pleasure Mr. Chope's *Carols for use in Church* during Christmas and Epiphany; the music is most carefully edited by Mr. Herbert Stephen Irons, who has introduced some original melodies, and there is a learned and interesting historical essay by Mr. Baring-Gould. This book should be found at all Christmas choir festivals. Mr. Chope has done well for those who may use his book in printing words and music together; and certainly most of his hymns, either for words or music, and often for both, are well adapted for the Church services."—*Saturday Review.*

"It contains nearly every one of the old traditional carols which are worth preserving (and these are all, with scarce an exception, admirably harmonised), and a large number of carols, either modern in words or music, or both, which are quite worthy, as a rule, of appearing with their time-honoured compeers. The work was composed mainly with a view to congregational use in church, and it takes in not only the festival tides of Christmas and Epiphany, and the Saints' days clustering round Christmas, but even the Conversion of S. Paul and the Purification. In many of the carols the composers have caught most admirably the form and spirit of the genuine old carol. There is also a learned and most interesting preface on the origin of carol-singing, and the customs connected therewith (which would alone make the book worth getting), by the Rev. S. Baring-Gould. We earnestly recommend it to the notice and adoption of our friends, more especially of the clergy, in the approaching and future Christmas seasons."—*Literary Churchman.*

"During the last few years carol-singing has been extensively revived. It had never, indeed, quite died out in our rural districts, in which roughly printed broadsides, with grotesque woodcuts, were, and are to this day, annually purchasable at 'the' village shop. These broadsides are issued from the neighbourhood of Seven Dials, in a type, or rather in a conglomeration of odd specimens of type, which would fairly shock the nerves of a good compositor; yet their circulation is enormous, and, if their printers cannot excite our admiration, they at least deserve our gratitude, for they have sustained the very existence of some of the most beautiful carols during a long period of neglect at the hands of musicians and men of letters. The revival of carolling has now reached such a point that hearty churchmen must needs bring their carol-book into the sacred precincts, and so make into an act of worship what was formerly considered only a recreation at a social gathering. All who have searched into the earliest known sources of English carols must have been struck with the excessive number of a secular character. Our immediate forefathers seem to have been more pleased to sing of the crackling log and bowl of beer, than to turn their thoughts to Bethlehem, and meditate on the Incarnation. Hence, a secular style of music has to a great extent become wedded even to those carols not containing any special allusion to social hilarity, and a want has been felt by many of a set of carols for Church use. To supply this want, Mr. Chope, already so well known as one of the earliest, if not the most successful labourer in the field of hymnody has issued this little book, in which some of the best-known traditional sacred carols are supplemented by a large collection of new tunes to new words, of various degrees of merit. The first modern carols which deserve special mention are 19,—a charming melody; 29,—quite certain to become a popular favourite; 34,—runs smoothly and calmly from the first note to the last. The Epiphany Carols are a noticeable feature in the book, and give it a special value;— 95 and 104 stand out pre-eminently for originality and sprightliness, and the fine old melody of 92 will be welcome to all. If space permitted we would gladly enter into further details; but enough has been said to show that Mr. Chope has done a real service by the publication of this book, and the reader will find on every page evident tokens of the care he has bestowed on it. The new compositions

## EXTRACTS FROM REVIEWS.

are, as a rule, remarkably good. Not the least valuable part of the work is the excellent historical essay by Mr. S. Baring-Gould; all lovers of carols will read it with great interest. The printing of both music and words is delightfully clear and readable."—*The Guardian.*

"We hail the appearance of this work with the highest satisfaction, and think that Mr. Chope has laid all lovers of carols, and indeed we may say all good Christians, under a lasting debt of gratitude by this admirable collection of carols, ancient and modern, which we strongly incline to think the public and unbiassed judges will agree with us in pronouncing at once the best and most copious by far which has yet appeared. A most interesting and erudite preface has been added by the Rev. S. Baring-Gould, embodying all that is most valuable as to what may be termed carol lore and history—a preface quite worthy of being printed as a separate paper. The collection consists of 112 pieces, of which 68 are modern, in some cases in music only, some in music and words—but in a great many the words have undergone considerable alterations.—The numbers just specified, and the best of the arrangements of the old carol tunes which we shall mention would alone make it worth while to obtain the book. The arrangements of old carols are all good."—*The Choir.*

"To those who are fond of Christmas carols—and who is not?—this book will prove a real treasure. Here are 112 carols, ancient and modern, the latter by some of the best composers of the present time. There is a learned introduction by the Rev. S. Baring-Gould, containing highly interesting matter. Of course, all such old favourites as 'God's dear Son,' 'The First Nowell,' &c., are here; and we have also some charming modern compositions which will stand well beside these, and will doubtless hold their own in years to come. In England, after the Reformation, when Latin hymns were abolished, carols were commonly sung in churches, as now in Cornwall, until Epiphany. To assist the further restoration of this pious use of our forefathers the present enlarged collection is put forth.

"At the time of the fourteenth and fifteenth centuries carol-singing seems to have been much in vogue, and we have many still extant of that period. In the times of the Tudors we have many examples of carols and carol-singing, and even the prices of carols, as 'To Sr. Mark for carolls for Christmass, and for 5 square Books, iijs. iiijd.' Soon after this, carol-singing and other cheerful observances were, as much as possible, suppressed by the Puritans.

"The carol, in a homely intelligent manner, brings the doctrine of the Incarnation home to simple minds, where sermons and hymns sometimes fail to do so. It would be well, therefore, if the Clergy of the Church of England would adopt the carol, and use it at Christmas-tide in their churches. For this purpose, as well as for those good-natured people who are seeking to make presents to musical friends, here is an admirable book ready to hand, which is certain to be welcome wherever it is introduced." *John Bull.*

"Mr. Chope, whose name is well-known among Church musicians as the editor of a popular tune-book and psalter, has given us in this work by far the most compendious collection we have yet seen of these seasonable songs. Mr. Chope has apparently ransacked the manuscripts of the past as diligently as he has secured the co-operation of the carol-writers of the present, and the result is a book of genuine musical interest, while it is also fitted for popular and congregational use. The words are for the most part singularly free from the quaint conceits which disfigure some of the older carols in other volumes, and the music is throughout very carefully edited. Whether the clergy generally will act on the editor's hint, and introduce a set of carols as a pendant to one or more of their Christmas services, remains to be seen; but the custom already obtains in a large number of parishes, and even those who do not approve of the 'use' will find the book admirably adapted for their school and congregational gatherings."—*English Churchman.*

Now ready, 248 pages, cloth lettered, red edges, 4s.

## CAROLS FOR USE IN CHURCH DURING CHRISTMAS AND EPIPHANY.
By R. R. CHOPE, M.A., Vicar of S. Augustine's, South Kensington, &c. The Music edited by HERBERT STEPHEN IRONS, late Organist of Southwell Minster. With an Introduction by S. BARING-GOULD, M.A., Rector of Lew Trenchard, author of "The Lives of the Saints," &c. In this Work there are Carols for Christmas Eve, Christmas Day, S. Stephen, S. John, Holy Innocents, New Year's Eve, New Year's Day, Circumcision, Epiphany, Sundays after Epiphany, Conversion of S. Paul, Purification of B. V. M. The Traditional Carols are from different counties and countries—the modern by well-known authors.

Applications for grants of Carols, Music or Words, should be sent to the Rev. R. R. CHOPE, Vicarage, 117, Queen's Gate, South Kensington, S.W., and should contain a stamped and addressed envelope for reply.

|   |   | s. | d. |   |   | s. | d. |
|---|---|---|---|---|---|---|---|
| A. | Cloth, gilt, FULL SCORE, expression marks, &c. | 4 | 0 | E. | TREBLE PART, in paper cover | 1 | 0 |
|   |   |   |   | F. | Ditto, cloth, gilt lettered | 1 | 6 |
| B. | Suitable for presents, in handsome binding, designed by Mr. Butterfield, full score | 7 | 6 | G. | Words only, ONE PENNY | 0 | 1 |
|   |   |   |   | H. | Words only, cloth gilt, special design, illustrated with copious Woodcuts | 1 | 6 |
| C. | Words only, in paper cover | 0 | 6 |   |   |   |   |
| D. | Words only, cloth, gilt lettered | 1 | 0 | K. | Full score, CHEAP EDITION | 2 | 0 |

London: METZLER and CO., Great Marlborough Street.
NOVELLO, EWER and CO., 1, Berners Street.

---

Cloth, 1s. 6d.

## THE CATECHIST; a Manual for use in Churches, at Confirmation Lectures, and at Home.
By R. R. CHOPE, M.A., Vicar of S. Augustine's, South Kensington. Fourth Edition.

London: SIMPKIN, MARSHALL and CO., Stationers' Hall Court.

---

Fifth Edition, 2d.

## AN ORDER FOR LAYING THE CORNER-STONE OF A NEW CHURCH.
Sanctioned for use by the Bishops of London, Oxford, Peterborough, S. Alban's, Salisbury, Bangor, and Llandaff. Compiled by R. R. CHOPE.

London: RIVINGTONS, Waterloo Place.

---

8vo., price 6d.

## OFFERTORY SENTENCES COMPLETE (twenty), with Music in full, for Organist and Choir.
By HERBERT STEPHEN IRONS, late Organist of Southwell Minster. One or more of these beautiful and effective sentences may be sung after the Priest has said the Offertory, or after the hymns at Mattins or Evensong, whilst the alms are being collected.

London: NOVELLO, EWER and CO., 1, Berners Street.

---

Price 3d.

## TE DEUM FOR FESTIVALS. From "Marbeck" and "La Feillée."
Arranged by H. FLEETWOOD SHEPPARD, M.A.
There can be no more melodious and appropriate music than this for a most difficult yet most glorious hymn of the Church. Excellent for Festivals of Choirs.

London: NOVELLO, EWER and CO., 1, Berners Street.

LONDON:
WILLIAM CLOWES AND SONS, LIMITED, TYPE-MUSIC AND GENERAL PRINTERS,
STAMFORD STREET AND CHARING CROSS.

www.ingramcontent.com/pod-product-compliance
Lightning Source LLC
Chambersburg PA
CBHW020757230426
43666CB00007B/739